Microsoft OFFICE for iPad

An Essential Guide to Microsoft Word,
Excel, PowerPoint, and OneDrive

TOM NEGRINO

Office for iPad
An Essential Guide to Microsoft Word, Excel, PowerPoint, and OneDrive
Tom Negrino

Peachpit Press
Find us on the web at: www.peachpit.com
To report errors, please send a note to errata@peachpit.com

Peachpit Press is a division of Pearson Education

Copyright © 2015 by Tom Negrino

Project Editor: Clifford Colby
Production Editor: Dennis Fitzgerald
Compositor: Danielle Foster
Indexer: Valerie Haynes Perry
Cover Design: Aren.Straiger
Interior Design: Mimi Heft

Notice of Rights

Notice of Liability

The information in this book is distributed on an "As Is" basis without warranty. While every precaution has been taken in the preparation of the book, neither the author nor Peachpit shall have any liability to any person or entity with respect to any loss or damage caused or alleged to be caused directly or indirectly by the instructions contained in this book or by the computer software and hardware products described in it.

Trademarks

Many of the designations used by manufacturers and sellers to distinguish their products are claimed as trademarks. Where those designations appear in this book, and Peachpit was aware of a trademark claim, the designations appear as requested by the owner of the trademark. All other product names and services identified throughout this book are used in editorial fashion only and for the benefit of such companies with no intention of infringement of the trademark. No such use, or the use of any trade name, is intended to convey endorsement or other affiliation with this book.

ISBN 13: 978-0-133-98870-3
ISBN 10: 0-133-98870-8

9 8 7 6 5 4 3 2 1

Printed and bound in the United States of America

This book was written in honor of the many members of my family and friends whose love and support helped me get through writing it at an especially distressing and difficult time in my life. My special appreciation to David and Care Morgenstern for their warm food and warmer friendship.

Most of all, I dedicate the book to my wife Dori, without whom I could not have made it.

About the Author

Tom Negrino is the author or co-author of nearly 50 books, covering such diverse topics as Microsoft Office, iCloud, OS X, Dreamweaver, JavaScript, Keynote, CSS, and more. He is a longtime contributor to *Macworld* and other magazines. He's lived in the Sonoma wine country with his wife and frequent collaborator, Dori Smith, since they fled the Los Angeles area in 1999.

Special Thanks to:

My project editor, Cliff Colby, who pitched this book to me and to management, shepherding the project across the finish line while still managing to overcome the difficulties inherent to any project that runs tight on time.

Thanks to Dennis Fitzgerald for taking care of running the production side.

I very much appreciate Dori Smith's assistance with editing and page proofing.

My thanks to the book's compositor, Danielle Foster, and thanks to Valerie Haynes Perry for the index.

Thanks as always to Peachpit's Nancy Ruenzel and Nancy Davis for their friendship and support.

Contents

GETTING STARTED

CHAPTER 1 **Understanding Office 365**   1

Using Office 365 2
Subscribing to Office 365 2
Understanding Office 365 components 4
Adding people to your Office 365 account 5
Storing Documents On and Off the Cloud. 7
Using the Correct File Formats. 9

CHAPTER 2 **Installing Software on Mobile Devices and Your Desktop**   11

Mobile Device Setup. 12
Downloading the Office apps. 12
Signing in to your account 14
Desktop Setup. 15
Installing Windows software 17
Installing Mac software 18

CHAPTER 3 **Setting Up OneDrive**   19

Setting up OneDrive on Your iPad 20
Installing OneDrive on Desktop Machines 22
Mac installation. 22
Windows installation 23
Running OneDrive for the First Time 24
Understanding OneDrive Folders. 27

MANAGING DOCUMENTS

CHAPTER 4 **Beginning with the Office Apps**   29

Creating New Documents. 30
Saving and Naming Documents 31
Opening Documents. 34
Pinning documents 36
Managing recent documents 37
Sharing Documents. 38

Printing Documents. 40

Introducing the Office for iPad Interface 41

CHAPTER 5 Working with Templates   43

Creating Documents from the Built-In Templates 44

Importing Templates from Desktop Versions of Office 48

Importing templates from Office 2013 in Windows. 49

Importing templates from Office 2011 for Mac 54

Importing Templates from Office Online 57

Duplicating saved documents 57

Saving Office Online templates with the desktop versions of Office. 62

CHAPTER 6 Using the OneDrive App   65

Introducing the OneDrive App. 66

Signing in to the OneDrive app 66

Touring the OneDrive app 68

Working with Folders 69

Creating folders 70

Renaming folders 73

Deleting and moving folders 75

Working with Files. 78

Viewing and opening Office files 78

Viewing and opening other files. 80

Renaming files. 83

Deleting and moving files. 84

Sharing Files and Folders 84

Sharing folders 85

Sharing files. 87

Refreshing Folders and Files. 88

Using the Other Tabs 89

Using Settings 90

CHAPTER 7 Editing Documents with Office Online   91

Using Office Online. 92

Creating a New Office Online Document. 94

Managing Office Online Documents 97

Opening documents. 98

Renaming and printing documents 99
Sharing documents 100
Editing documents 100
Accessing earlier versions of documents 100

Sharing Your Office Online Documents 101
Sharing via email 102
Sharing with a link on social media 103
Sharing by embedding a document in a Web page 104

Managing Applications and Services 106

WORKING WITH WORD

CHAPTER 8 **Working with Text**   107

Adding Text 108
Entering and editing text 109
Styling text 110

Working with Lists 112

Finding and Replacing Text 114

Getting Word Counts 115

CHAPTER 9 **Formatting and Collaboration**   117

Working with the Ruler 118
Using the Ruler to set indents 118
Using the Ruler to set tabs 119

Working with Headers and Footers 121

Inserting Page Numbers 122

Document Markup and Review 123
Working with comments 124
Tracking changes 125

CHAPTER 10 **Changing Document Layout**   127

Working with Margins 128

Changing Your Virtual Paper 129

Adding Page and Section Breaks 130

Adding Columns 132

USING EXCEL

CHAPTER 11 **Working with Worksheets**   **135**

Getting Started with Excel 136

Selecting and Entering Data. 139

   Entering data 140

   Filling data 142

Working with Rows and Columns 143

   Selecting rows and columns 143

   Inserting rows and columns 144

Freezing Panes 145

CHAPTER 12 **Working with Worksheet Data**   **147**

Formatting Worksheet Items. 148

   Formatting appearance. 148

   Formatting number values 151

   Copying formats 152

Building Formulas 153

Using the Formula Bar 155

Linking Worksheets 157

CHAPTER 13 **Building Charts**   **159**

Creating Charts. 160

Formatting Chart Styles 164

Applying Chart Layouts. 166

Switching Chart Axes 167

MAKING PRESENTATIONS WITH POWERPOINT

CHAPTER 14 **Building Presentations**   **169**

Importing Existing Presentations 170

   Watch for pitfalls 171

   Fix problems 173

Creating Presentations on iPad. 175

CHAPTER 15 **Working with Slides**   **177**

Modifying Slides 178

   Changing slide order 178

   Duplicating slides 179

Hiding slides 180

Deleting slides 181

Working with Text 181

Styling text 181

Copying styles. 183

Inserting text boxes 184

Adding Tables 185

Adding Images 187

Creating Shapes 189

CHAPTER 16 **Adding Transitions and Presenting**   **191**

Add Slide Transitions. 192

Preflight Your Show. 194

Give the Presentation 196

Preparing to present. 196

Making the hardware connection 197

Control the Presentation. 200

Playing the presentation 200

Marking up a slide 201

GETTING ORGANIZED WITH ONENOTE

CHAPTER 17 **Working with OneNote**   **203**

Understanding OneNote. 204

Capturing Notes 206

Capturing image notes. 208

Inserting tables 210

Inserting to-do lists 211

Styling Text Notes. 212

Sharing from OneNote 213

CHAPTER 18 **Organizing Your Notes**   **215**

Working with Notebooks 216

Working with Sections. 219

Working with Pages. 220

Finding Notes 222

Index 223

CHAPTER 1

Understanding Office 365

Welcome to *Office for iPad!* In the world of work and productivity software, Microsoft Office has become, for better or worse, the standard by which other productivity software must be judged. That's not to say that other word processing, spreadsheet, and presentation programs can't hold their own in comparison with Microsoft Office. Apple's own iWork suite (consisting of Pages, Numbers, and Keynote), for example, has much to recommend it and offers Microsoft Office compatibility as well.

Still, a large segment of the business market relies on Microsoft Office and expects it to be available on every hardware platform. That's one reason why the introduction, in early 2014, of the main Microsoft Office apps for the iPad was greeted with such excitement. For the first time, Microsoft Office documents could be created, viewed, and edited in native formats on the iPad, bringing the Office experience to Apple's tablet, the popularity of which far outstrips that of tablets running the Android or Windows operating systems.

This book focuses on using the five Office apps that were available for the iPad at the time I wrote this book: Word, Excel, PowerPoint, OneNote, and OneDrive. I show you how to work collaboratively with your Office documents, not just with other people, but also with your other installations of Office on your other machines. In this book, you see how these touch-enabled apps differ from the desktop versions and how working with OneDrive—Microsoft's cloud storage product—ensures safe, effortless saving and backup of your work.

Using Office 365

The most important thing you need to understand about the Microsoft Office apps for iPad is that to get most work done with them, you need a subscription to Office 365, which I discuss in the next section.

You can download all the Office apps from the App Store for free, but until you sign in to your Office 365 account, you can only read Office documents on your iPad—not change them. Without a subscription, you can use Word on the iPad to read documents and Excel to review spreadsheets, give a presentation with PowerPoint, and print documents from any of the apps. But you need an Office 365 subscription to edit, save, or create Word, Excel, or PowerPoint documents.

▶ **TIP** The exception, even though it's part of the Office 365 suite, is Microsoft OneNote, which is free to download and use with or without an Office 365 subscription.

Subscribing to Office 365

To get started subscribing to Office 365, follow these steps:

1. Go to http://office.microsoft.com (1.1).

   The first thing you need to do is decide what subscription level of Office 365 is right for you and whether you want to pay for that subscription on a monthly or annual basis.

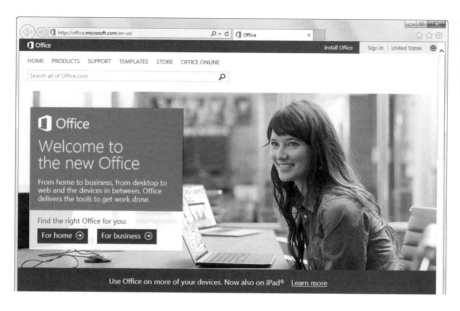

1.1 The Office site is where you get started with your Office 365 subscription and manage it when you complete the subscription process.

2. Click the For Home or For Business button and then review the different plans.

Microsoft has designed different plans for different types of subscribers:

- **Home:** For this book, I subscribed to Office 365 Home—one of the most popular plans, designed for sharing Office 365 within a family or a very small business—so the book focuses on using that plan. For $10 per month, the Home plan gives you access to the full Office 365 experience for up to five people, including access to the desktop versions of Microsoft Office for Mac or Windows; the ability to install the Office apps on tablets and smartphones; access to Office Online; and 60 minutes of Skype calls per month to mobile and landline phones in selected countries.

- **Business:** The Office 365 Business plans, in addition to the Microsoft Office versions for desktop and mobile devices, also allow Windows PCs that normally don't have the Office programs installed to use them via a streaming service called Office on Demand. The plans also provide many business collaboration features. Several Business plans are available, with prices depending on the number of users in your company and charged on a yearly basis.

- **University:** If you're a college student, you can subscribe to Office 365 University, which costs $80 for four years—a significant savings. It gives you access to desktop and tablet versions of the Office apps, 27 GB of OneDrive storage, and 60 minutes of Skype calls per month to mobile and landline phones in selected countries.

3. When you've chosen a plan, click the Buy Now button, and run through the checkout process.

   Each plan has its own checkout and signup process, but all the plans provide a confirmation email with instructions on how to complete Office 365 setup. Follow the instructions given in the confirmation email.

Understanding Office 365 components

When you subscribe to Office 365, you gain access to a lot of software and services. In this book, I focus on the Office apps that run on the iPad, but you get much more (depending on the nature of your Office 365 subscription):

- The Office apps for the iPad.

- OneDrive software for Windows or Mac that allows you to access your OneDrive, Microsoft's cloud storage service, from your desktop machines and integrates the desktop versions of Microsoft Office OneDrive (I discuss OneDrive in "Storing Documents On and Off the Cloud" later in this chapter).

- Some amount of storage (typically, 20 GB to 30 GB) on OneDrive.

- The latest versions of Microsoft Office for Mac and Windows.

  ▶ **NOTE** At press time, the latest versions were Microsoft Office 2013 for Windows and Microsoft Office 2011 for Mac. In Office for Windows, you get Word, Excel, PowerPoint, Outlook, OneNote, Access, and Publisher. In Office for Mac, you get Word, Excel, PowerPoint, Outlook, and OneNote. Microsoft promises that you'll have access to the latest versions as long as your Office 365 subscription is active.

- Office Online versions of some Office applications that run entirely in a browser. These apps aren't full-featured versions, but they work similarly and are powerful enough to allow you to make quick edits and touchups of your documents stored in OneDrive. Word Online, for example, allows you to add and style text (1.2); more advanced features such as adding columns and dealing with tracked changes are left to more robust versions of Word.

Office Online includes limited versions of Word, Excel, PowerPoint, and OneNote, as well as the People contact manager, the Calendar service, and the Outlook.com email service. I discuss using Office Online in Chapter 7.

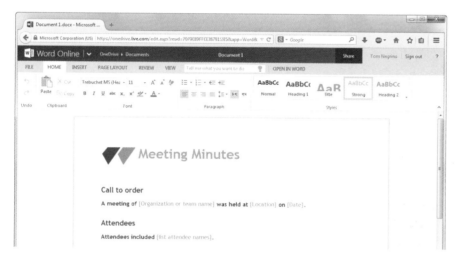

1.2 Word Online, running in a browser, is fairly capable, but it's better used for simpler, quicker edits than for heavy-duty work.

Adding people to your Office 365 account

After you subscribe to Office 365, you need to add people to your Office 365 account. The example in this section is for the Home subscription (see "Subscribing to Office 365" earlier in this chapter), but other plans are similar or are handled for you by your Office 365 administrator.

To begin adding people to your Office 365 Home account, follow these steps:

1. In a browser, go to http://office.microsoft.com.

2. Click the Sign In button at the top of the screen (1.3).

1.3 Click the Sign In button to get started administering your Office 365 account.

3. When prompted, enter the email address for your Microsoft account (1.4), and click Next.

1.4 Begin by entering the email address for your Microsoft account.

4. Enter the password for your Microsoft Account on the next screen; then click Next.

   You return to the main Office site, where the Sign In button is replaced by a pop-up menu labeled with your name.

5. From the pop-up menu, choose My Account (1.5).

   On your account screen, below the Share Your Subscription Benefits heading, is a list of people who are signed up, as well as empty slots (1.6). You can see who has accepted your invitation and who hasn't yet accepted it (marked as Pending).

1.5 Choose My Account to get to your administration page.

1.6 You can see which users have accepted your Office 365 invitation and which are pending.

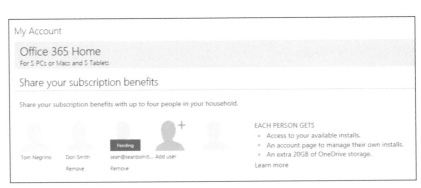

6. To add a user, click Add User; in the next screen, enter his or her email address and then click Send Invite (1.7).

That user receives an email invitation to share your subscription. When he or she accepts your invitation, you're notified via email. The invitation expires after 30 days, and again, you're notified via email.

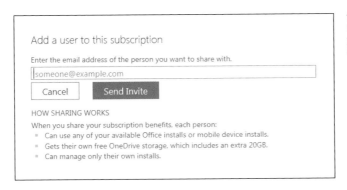

1.7 Begin your invitation by entering your new user's email address.

Each person who shares your subscription has his or her own Microsoft account and login information. Each user can choose what combination of software installations to take advantage of, and each user has a separate allocation of OneDrive cloud storage (see the next section).

Storing Documents On and Off the Cloud

Apple's odd notions of security and file management on the iPad and iPhone, especially because they try to hide the file system from users, make working with documents on those devices more difficult. Typically, each app on an iPad has access only to its own documents, with the exception of tightly controlled, systemwide shared files such as photos. You can think of each app as being locked in its own silo with its documents, with hard walls between programs (1.8). Files that are stored in the iPad's internal storage can be accessed only by the apps that created and saved them. This arrangement is in direct contrast to OS X and Windows. In those operating systems generally, any program has access to most of the file system, and users can choose to save documents in any folders they prefer.

This file separation is related to another problem with apps designed to run on mobile devices: You need some way to get the documents off the devices for backup and sharing. Apple wants developers to use its iCloud service, but many developers have discovered that iCloud is buggy and difficult to use.

Microsoft has chosen to build and use its own cloud storage service, called OneDrive (formerly SkyDrive). OneDrive is built into all the Office for iPad apps, and a separate OneDrive app allows you to manage the folders and files in your cloud storage (1.9).

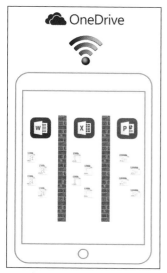

1.8 Files stored on the iPad can be accessed only by the apps that created them.

1.9 The OneDrive app on your iPad lets you manage any of the folders and files in your OneDrive storage.

Keep in mind a couple of things about the OneDrive app:

- It has access only to the files stored in OneDrive. Each of the Office apps, however, can store documents locally on the iPad *or* in OneDrive.

- The OneDrive app has no access to the Office apps' local iPad storage.

I look into the differences between local and cloud storage in more detail in Chapter 6.

▶ **NOTE** Each of the Office 365 apps has access to OneDrive via Wi-Fi, but even OneDrive doesn't have access to documents in an app's private storage. That's one reason why it's a good idea to store your documents in OneDrive rather than on the iPad whenever possible.

What's the Cloud, Anyway?

Cloud is an almost ubiquitous, poorly understood buzzword. It's even the basis for popular culture: A 2014 comedy movie called *Sex Tape* involves a sexy video inadvertently uploaded to the cloud by a married couple, who attempt to get the video removed before it besmirches their reputations. One of the characters even shouts in a panic, "Nobody understands the cloud! It's a mystery!"

Well, it's not *that* mysterious. Cloud storage is simply a bunch of hard drives (approximately a zillion) sitting in servers inside data centers run by many companies and available to you over the Internet. Your cloud storage provider—whether it be Microsoft, Apple, Google, Dropbox, or any of the many others—gives you software that allows you to store your files and folders on those hard drives. Depending on the software, your files are saved manually or automatically and can be distributed to different devices, again manually or automatically.

One benefit of cloud storage is that your files aren't held in only one place (such as your iPad), so if something bad happens to your iPad (such as theft, fire, or malicious toddlers), you can simply replace your hardware, restore your files from the cloud, and get right back to work. Another benefit is that any of your devices signed in to your cloud storage account has access to the same set of files and folders, making for easy sharing with yourself and easy collaboration with co-workers.

Just remember not to upload your sex tapes. That's never going to end well.

Using the Correct File Formats

Microsoft Office has been around for a long time, and over the years, it has accumulated many file formats, all of which are for Microsoft Office. But the current versions of Microsoft Office programs, while reading some of the older versions of the file formats, save files in the latest versions of the formats.

On the iPad, files that were saved in older formats open in a compatibility mode; these files must converted before you can edit and save the documents. An iPad program notifies you when this situation occurs (1.10).

Normally, conversion isn't a problem, but if some of your colleagues use old versions of Microsoft Office for Windows or Mac, they may need to install Service Packs or upgrade to newer versions to read the documents you work on with Office 365.

All versions of Office 365 save files in the latest file formats, known as the Office Open XML Document formats and listed in **Table 1.1**.

Table 1.1 Microsoft Office File Formats

Application	Older File Extensions	Office 365 File Extensions
Word	.doc, .dot	.docx, .docm, .dotx
Excel	.xls, .xlt	.xlsx, .xlsm, .xltx
PowerPoint	.ppt, .pot, .pps	.pptx, .pptm, .potx, .ppsx

In the file managers of the individual iPad apps, as well as in the OneDrive app, you can see the differences between old and new file formats (1.11).

1.11 The OneDrive file manager shows you which files have older and current file formats.

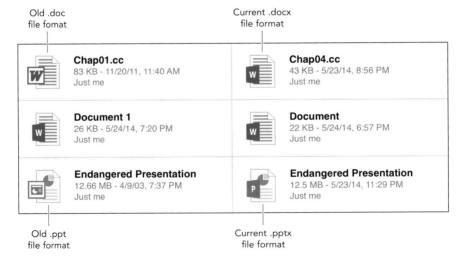

Old .doc file fomat

Current .docx file format

Old .ppt file format

Current .pptx file format

CHAPTER 2

Installing Software on Mobile Devices and Your Desktop

Microsoft Office 365 is software that (for the purposes of this book) lives in three places:

- The Office apps on your iPad

- The version of Office for Windows or for Mac that you can access as part of your Office 365 subscription

- The part that ties your mobile and desktop devices together: the cloud component, consisting of your OneDrive online storage and the Web-based versions of the Office applications

Taken together, these three places allow you to use Office 365 to get your work done almost anywhere.

In this chapter, you find out how to install the Office apps on your iPad, as well as how to access and install the Windows or Mac software on your desktop machine. You hold off on installing OneDrive until Chapter 3.

Mobile Device Setup

The first thing you need to do is download the Office apps from the App Store. You can do that by using the App Store app on your iPad, or you can use iTunes to access the iTunes Store, download the apps to your Mac or Windows PC, and then sync them to your iPad via USB. It's easier to download and install the apps right on the iPad with the App Store app, so I show you how in the next section.

Downloading the Office apps

You need five Office apps for this book—Microsoft Word for iPad, Microsoft Excel for iPad, Microsoft PowerPoint for iPad, Microsoft OneNote for iPad, and OneDrive—and you download them in this section.

▶ **NOTE** Before you start, make sure that you're on a reasonably fast Wi-Fi connection, as the main Office apps are large for iPad apps (approximately 200 MB each).

To download the Office apps on your iPad, follow these steps:

1. Find and tap the App Store app's icon.

    In the App Store, the easiest way to find the Office 365 apps is to do a search.

2. Tap the search box in the top-right corner, which brings up the onscreen keyboard, and type **Microsoft**.

    As you type, search results appear (2.1).

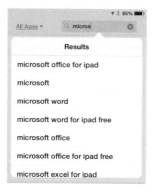

2.1 Search for the Microsoft Office apps.

3. Tap one of the results in the pop-up list, and your search results appear (2.2).

Next to each app icon, the download button that usually shows the price of an app displays the word *Free* for each of the Office 365 apps. Although the apps are free to download, unless you have a Office 365 subscription, all you can do with them is view Microsoft Office documents; you can't create or edit documents.

2.2 The App Store shows the Office 365 apps are free to download to your iPad.

4. Tap the Free button to begin your download.

When you tap it, the Free button is replaced by a download progress icon. Then, when the app finishes downloading, the button changes to Open. You don't have to wait for one app to finish downloading before you begin to download the next.

5. Repeat the download process until you've downloaded all five of the apps you'll be using in this book.

You may need to scroll through the search-results list (refer to 2.1) or even perform a new search to find all the apps.

When you've downloaded all the Office 365 apps, they appear individually on your iPad's *Springboard,* which is the actual name that the iPad uses for its desktop. You can leave the apps that way, or you can put them all in a folder. To put them in a folder, tap and hold each of the app icons until they begin to wiggle, and drag them on top of one another to create a folder. Then tap the folder's name field and enter a name. When you're done, all the apps are neatly grouped together (2.3).

2.3 You don't have to, but I like to group all my Office apps in a single folder.

Signing in to your account

The Office apps aren't quite ready for use yet; to get down to work, you need to sign in to your Microsoft Office 365 account (which is usually the same as your general Microsoft account). You can do that in most of the Office apps, and the other apps recognize your sign-in so you don't have to repeat it. The exception is the OneDrive app, which uses an independent sign-in from the other apps but still uses the same Microsoft account.

To sign in to Office 365, just tap the Word, Excel, PowerPoint, or OneNote icon. You'll be asked to type the email account associated with your Microsoft account, the email and your password, or both. If the Sign In sheet doesn't appear, tap the Sign In button in the top-left corner of the app (2.4), which forces the Sign In sheet to appear (2.5). Enter the information the sheet asks for and then tap Next (or tap the Return key on the onscreen keyboard). You'll be prompted for your password on the next screen.

When you've signed in correctly, any cloud storage services, folders, and documents that you previously created appear (2.6).

2.4 If necessary, tap the Sign In button that appears in the top-left corner of each Office app.

2.5 Type your email address, and tap Next.

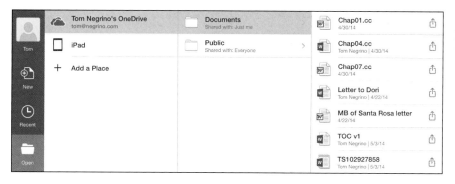

2.6 After you sign in, the contents of your cloud storage become visible.

Microsoft's Many Cloud Storage Services

The storage locations supported by Microsoft Office for iPad are two kinds of cloud services: OneDrive and OneDrive for Business (which comes with subscription plans for Office 365 that are specifically oriented to businesses large and small). OneDrive for Business also provides a system administrator, various access controls for workgroups, folders, and document sharing, all of which are outside of the scope of this book.

You can also connect Office 365 to SharePoint storage locations that can be accessed over a local network or over the Internet. SharePoint is Microsoft's Web-based collaboration software, with many features. Again, it's designed for businesses and requires a system administrator, so it's beyond this book's scope. If you're using the iPad apps in a SharePoint environment, speak to your sysadmin for detailed instructions on storing your Office 365 documents in SharePoint locations.

Desktop Setup

After you've got the Office apps installed on your iPad, it's time to turn to your desktop machines. The Office 365 subscription gives you access to the latest desktop versions of Microsoft Office, which are Microsoft Office 2013 for Windows and Microsoft Office 2011 for the Mac at this writing. If Microsoft updates the desktop versions of Microsoft Office while your subscription is active, you get to update to the latest and greatest versions for free.

You can download the desktop versions of Microsoft Office from your Office 365 account page. To do so, follow these steps:

1. Go to http://office.microsoft.com (2.7), and click the Sign In link at the top of the screen.

2.7 Download desktop software from the Office Web site.

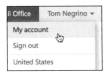

2.8 After you sign in, this pop-up menu allows you to get to your account settings.

2. When prompted, enter your Microsoft account username (almost always an email address) and your password; then click the Sign In button.

   You return to the main Office page, where your name now appears in the top-right corner as a pop-up menu (2.8).

3. Choose My Account from the pop-up menu.

   After a brief delay, your My Account screen appears (2.9).

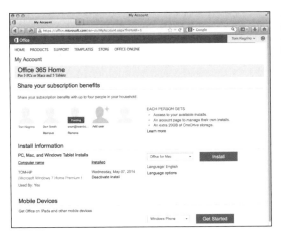

2.9 Your Account screen gives you an overview of your subscription benefits and what software installations are in use.

As I mention in Chapter 1, depending on the subscription plan you have for Office 365, you see one, five, or more users. While writing this book, I used an Office 365 Home subscription, which I can share with five people. Each of those people has his or her own sign-in details and separate access to all versions (tablet, Windows, Mac, and Web) of the Office applications.

Installing Windows software

To install the Windows Office software, go to http://office.microsoft.com, sign in, and then follow these steps:

1. On your My Account screen (refer to 2.9 earlier in this chapter), scroll down to the Install Information section, choose Office for Windows from the pop-up menu (2.10), and then click the Install button.

    A small installation program downloads to your Windows PC.

2.10 Choose the Windows versions of Office to start the download to your PC.

2. After the installation program downloads, open your browser's Downloads folder to find the installer program (2.11); double-click the installer program and then follow its prompts to install Office 2013.

    The full installer program downloads and installs the entire Office suite. The process takes quite a while, though you can begin using the core programs in the suite before the entire installation has run its course.

    ▶ **NOTE** Microsoft Office 2013 includes Word, Excel, PowerPoint, OneNote, Outlook, and two programs that aren't available for the Mac: Publisher (desktop publishing) and Access (database).

2.11 Double-click the installer program (which probably will be named something different) to begin the full installation process.

Installing Mac software

To install the Mac Office software, go to http://office.microsoft.com, sign in, and then follow these steps:

1. On your My Account screen (refer to 2.9 earlier in this chapter), scroll down to the Install Information section, choose Office for Mac from the pop-up menu (2.12), and then click the Install button.

2.12 To install Office for Mac, choose it from the pop-up menu. Note that I've already installed a copy of Office for Windows.

Unlike the Office for Windows installation (see the preceding section), the Mac installation downloads a Mac installer (2.13)—a standard .dmg package containing the entire Office 2011 suite, which is approximately 1 GB.

MicrosoftOffice201
1.dmg
1.01 GB

2.13 Double-click the Mac installer to get to the actual Office installer program.

2. When the installer is downloaded, locate it in your Downloads folder, and double-click its icon.

    A Finder window opens, displaying the Office Installer program (2.14).

2.14 Double-click the Office Installer to place your copy of Microsoft Office 2011 on your Mac.

3. Double-click that program to bring up the familiar Macintosh installer.

4. Follow the multiple onscreen prompts to finish installing Microsoft Office 2011 for Mac.

    After installation, you'll find the Office suite in the Microsoft Office 2011 folder inside your Applications folder.

CHAPTER 3

Setting Up
OneDrive

When you have Office on your iPad and on your desktop machines, you need some way to easily share the files through a cloud service so you can work on your documents anywhere. Apple has made the process difficult, however, by implementing unusual security requirements, hiding files and folders on iPads, and making it difficult for different apps to share files. Apple suggests that developers use its own iCloud service, but many developers find using iCloud for shared storage to be difficult to implement, subject to arbitrary changes in Apple's policies, and technically not ready for prime time. A large number of developers have turned to the popular Dropbox shared storage application, which works well on almost every platform, but Microsoft isn't interested in tethering Office—one of its crown jewels, after all—to an outside developer.

Microsoft's solution was to create its own cloud storage service, OneDrive (previously called SkyDrive). As with Dropbox, you can install OneDrive software on desktop and mobile machines, creating a special OneDrive folder on the desktop machines. Files and folders within the OneDrive folder you create and modify on one device are automatically synchronized on all the other devices.

On the iPad, all Office apps have access to the OneDrive documents in the cloud, and these documents can be downloaded to the iPad for viewing or editing.

In this chapter, you see how to install OneDrive on the iPad and on Mac and Windows machines. You also see how the OneDrive system allows you to work with your documents freely no matter which device you're using.

▶ **TIP** This book talks about installing the Office apps on the iPad, but the iPad isn't the only tablet that can run Office. Microsoft's own Surface Pro 2 and 3, as well as tablets from other manufacturers that run Windows, use the Windows versions of the Office 2013 suite.

Setting up OneDrive on Your iPad

If you completed the installation instructions in Chapter 2, you installed the OneDrive app along with the rest of the Office 365 apps, so now you just have to start it up and get signed in. Tap the OneDrive app icon; then tap the Sign In button that appears (3.1). On the following screen, which asks for your Microsoft account and password, enter that information; then tap either Sign In or the Go button on the onscreen keyboard.

If you haven't already done so, you'll be prompted to turn on Camera Backup, which automatically uploads the Camera Roll photos on your iPad to One-Drive (3.2). In return, Microsoft awards you an extra 3 GB of storage space in your OneDrive account. It seems like a good deal, especially as photos get uploaded only when your iPad is connected via Wi-Fi. Tap OK to accept, or tap the teeny-tiny No Thanks button if you don't want to use this service.

3.1 Use the iPad's OneDrive app to sign in to your Microsoft account.

3.2 Choose whether to enable the Camera Backup feature.

When sign-in is complete, you see your online folders (3.3). I discuss these folders later in this chapter.

3.3 The OneDrive app shows you all the folders in your OneDrive cloud storage.

Everybody Wants to Hold Your Photos

One thing many freemium cloud services have in common is they want to make it easy for you to store your photos with them. The idea is that because a photo collection is a large, unwieldy amount of data, if you store your photos on a particular service, you're more likely to stick with that service in the future. To that end, OneDrive, iCloud, Dropbox, and other services have a convenient feature that automatically uploads the contents of the Camera Roll on your iOS device.

Some services give you various incentives to choose them for your photo backup needs. Any time you take a picture on an iOS device, for example, iCloud automatically pushes it to all your other iOS devices, Apple's photo organization and editing programs (iPhoto and Aperture), and stores your most recent 1,000 photos in the cloud and on your devices for 30 days. ICloud also allows you to create shared photo streams with people you choose.

Dropbox has a automatic photo-uploading feature (again, from your Camera Roll) and provides its own iOS and Android app, Carousel, to help you organize and share your photos. Using Carousel or enabling photo uploading via the Dropbox app adds 3 GB of space to your free Dropbox storage.

The granddaddy of online photo storage and organization, Flickr, offers a whopping 1 TB of free photo storage, but you have to do most of the organizing and uploading yourself.

Installing OneDrive on Desktop Machines

You must install OneDrive software on each of your Mac and Windows machines that you want to have access to the service. When you do so, and when the software is running, you designate a folder to serve as the OneDrive folder. From then on, the contents of that folder (files and folders) are automatically synchronized, so changes made on one device are automatically pushed to all the other devices attached to your OneDrive account.

Getting started with OneDrive is virtually identical on Mac and Windows, so I cover the process in "Running OneDrive for the First Time" later in this section.

Mac installation

Installing the OneDrive software on the Mac is easy, as the software is available in the Mac App Store. The OneDrive app requires OS X 10.7.3 (Lion) or later, so chances are good that your machine is compatible.

To install the software, follow these steps:

1. Choose App Store from the Apple menu.

2. Enter **OneDrive** in the search field in the App Store's top-right corner.

3. Click OneDrive in the search results.

4. In the resulting OneDrive detail page, click the Install button (3.4).

3.4 On the Mac, click the Install button for the OneDrive application in the Mac App Store.

5. If you're asked to do so, enter your Apple ID and password.

The App Store installs the OneDrive program in your Applications folder.

Windows installation

If you're running Windows 8.1 or later, you don't need to do anything, because OneDrive is built in.

▶ **NOTE** If you're still running Windows XP, you're out of luck; the Windows installer won't run in that ancient and no-longer-supported operating system. You really should upgrade, you know.

To install OneDrive for Windows 8, Windows 7, and earlier versions, follow these steps:

1. Go to https://onedrive.live.com (3.5) in a browser.

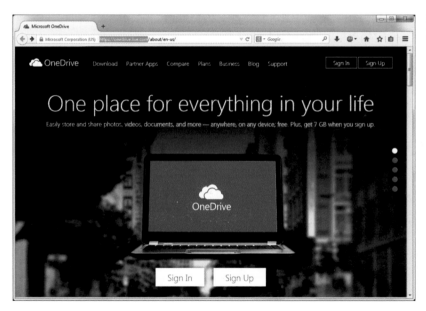

3.5 Install OneDrive from the OneDrive Web site.

2. Click the Download link at the top of the page, then click Choose Your Device (3.6) to expand the menu.

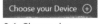

3.6 Choose the correct software for your device.

3. Choose PC | Mac from the Choose Your Device menu; then scroll down to see the revealed options (3.7).

3.7 Find the download link for your operating system.

4. Click the Download OneDrive for Windows link.

   The installer program downloads.

5. When the installer program is downloaded, open and run it from your browser's Downloads folder.

Running OneDrive for the First Time

Here's how to run OneDrive for the first time:

1. Depending on your platform, do one of the following:

   - On a Mac, open the Applications folder and double-click the One-Drive icon (3.8).

   - In Windows 7 and earlier versions, the installation program begins when you open the installer program from your browser's Downloads folder.

   On either platform, the OneDrive splash screen appears (3.9).

2. Click Get Started.

3. In the next screen, enter the username and password for your Microsoft account; then click Sign In (3.10).

OneDrive

3.8 On the Mac, get started by double-clicking the OneDrive icon in your Applications folder.

3.9 The Windows OneDrive splash screen (similar to the Mac version).

3.10 Enter the username and password for your Microsoft account.

4. In the next screen, specify the location of your OneDrive folder:

   - *Windows:* The folder is created at C:\Users*username*\OneDrive (**3.11**). You can accept that default location by clicking the Next button, or click Change and navigate to your preferred location.

   - *Mac:* On the Mac (**3.12**), you have two tasks, one of which is optional. You can click the Open at Login check box to make sure that OneDrive is always available to you. (I recommend that you do.) You must choose the location of your OneDrive folder. (I suggest you place it within the Documents folder.)

3.11 Windows OneDrive setup creates a default location for your OneDrive folder, but you can change it in this screen.

3.12 On the Mac, you must pick your OneDrive folder and may choose to have OneDrive open at login.

5. When you're done choosing the location of your OneDrive folder, click the Next button.

   On both platforms, the next screen allows you to sync only certain folders within your OneDrive folder (3.13). Your sync settings can be changed for each machine on which you have OneDrive installed. If, for example, you don't want to clutter your laptop with the contents of the Camera Roll on your iPad, you can click the Choose Folders to Sync button and exclude the Pictures folder.

6. For now, accept the default sync settings, which will synchronize all files and folders on your OneDrive; then, click the Next button (Windows) or Done button (Mac).

   In Windows, you still have one more choice to make: whether to allow your OneDrive account to access files on your PC that you forgot to put inside your OneDrive folder (3.14).

7. If you're comfortable with the security implications of this choice, accept the default setting (Let Me Use OneDrive to Fetch Any of My Files on This PC) and then click Done, or clear the check box and then click Done.

3.13 You can use this screen to choose which OneDrive folders you want to exclude from synchronization.

3.14 In Windows, you can use OneDrive to access the contents of your entire PC.

When you complete installation, the OneDrive folder on your machine begins downloading and synchronizing the contents of your OneDrive cloud storage.

▶ **TIP** You can't rename or move your OneDrive folder on either platform; if you do, OneDrive stops working. The only way to get it working again is to uninstall OneDrive, reinstall it, and configure the new location as the OneDrive folder.

Understanding OneDrive Folders

Your OneDrive folder acts just like any other folder, with one exception. Any additions, deletions, or file edits in any of the OneDrive folders on any of your machines are automatically synchronized to all the other machines connected to your OneDrive account—that is, unless you've set particular folders to be excluded from syncing, as discussed in "Running OneDrive for the First Time" earlier in this chapter. You can freely add files and folders to the OneDrive folder, and those files are made available to your other devices.

▶ **TIP** Individual files that you add to a OneDrive folder can't exceed 2 GB.

Another hidden benefit is that the files you work on inside your OneDrive folder are automatically backed up to as many devices as you have attached to your OneDrive account, with no extra effort on your part. Because you can never really have too many backups, using OneDrive should add to your peace of mind.

Keep in mind that the individual Office for iPad apps can read only the kinds of files that they're compatible with and that those file compatibilities may not be the same as those of the desktop versions of Office. In a desktop version of Office, you may be used to opening an Excel worksheet with Word so you can incorporate the worksheet into your document. The iPad version of Word, however, can open only Word documents, and some limitations apply (see Chapter 1). You'll be able to open that Excel worksheet in Excel for iPad, of course, but the file manager in each iPad app shows only compatible documents in the OneDrive folders.

On the other hand, the OneDrive app for iPad can see *all* the documents in each of the OneDrive folders, and you can use that app to preview documents and open them in their respective iPad apps. For more on that feature, see Chapter 8.

For now, I'll discuss the default folders (created by the OneDrive service) that appear in your OneDrive folder and their intended uses (3.15):

- **Documents** is for whatever files you want to put in it. You could create subfolders to segregate different types of Office documents, for example, or set up project folders within the main Documents folder.

- **Pictures** usually contains a Camera Roll folder, in which you'll find all the automatically uploaded pictures from your iOS device.

- **Public** contains documents that you've chosen to share with everyone. After moving documents to this folder you must share a link to them by sending an email or by getting and posting a link to social media or your blog. For more information about sharing documents, see Chapter 7.

- **Favorites** and **Shared Favorites,** created by default, are vestigial folders originally intended for a service that Microsoft no longer offers. I expect that sooner or later, the OneDrive software will be updated and these folders will no longer be created automatically. In the meantime, you can safely delete them so that they don't clutter your OneDrive folder.

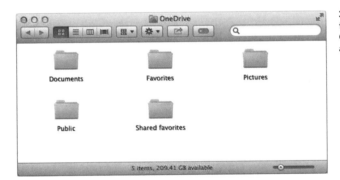

3.15 The default folders inside your OneDrive folder on a Mac.

CHAPTER 4

Beginning with the Office Apps

In this chapter, you get started working with the Office for iPad apps. You see how to create new documents and save them, to either your OneDrive cloud storage or to your local iPad storage. You also learn how to share and print documents from the iPad apps.

And because this is the chapter where you begin working with documents on the iPad, you also learn about how to work in the Office apps that have been adapted for use in a touch environment like the iPad, rather than the versions of Office you've been used to using for years, which rely on menus, a keyboard, and mouse.

Creating New Documents

Working with any documents in the Office for iPad apps requires that you be signed in to your Office 365 account, and I'm going to make the assumption in this and subsequent chapters that you have already done so, as discussed in Chapter 2.

To create a new blank document in Word, Excel, or PowerPoint, you follow the same basic procedure. Follow these steps:

1. On the iPad, tap the icon for the app you want to work in. We're using Word in this example.

   The app opens to the file manager, and is set to the Open tab by default (4.1).

4.1 You use the file manager to access files from either your OneDrive or the iPad's internal storage.

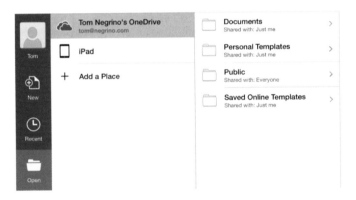

2. Tap the New icon.

   The New screen appears (4.2), and contains a blank document template at its upper-left corner, as well as some other templates (we'll discuss those other templates in Chapter 5).

3. Tap New Blank Document (in Word), New Blank Workbook (Excel), or Office Light (PowerPoint) template.

   ▶ **TIP** In PowerPoint, there really isn't a concept of a completely blank document, since every presentation comes with styles, master slides, and slide formats. The Office Light template is a stark, predominantly white template that is as close as you can get to blank in PowerPoint.

   The new document opens, ready for editing (4.3).

4.2 Use the first listed template to create a blank document.

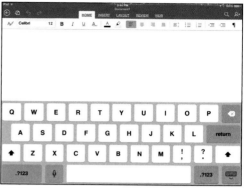

4.3 Word has created a new document, ready for you to fill it with your brilliance.

In 4.3, you can see that the onscreen keyboard is displayed. That was because I didn't have an external Bluetooth keyboard connected to my iPad at the time. When a Bluetooth keyboard is connected, the onscreen keyboard doesn't appear.

Saving and Naming Documents

From one standpoint, you don't need to do anything to save your Office for iPad documents, because from the moment it's created it's autosaved every few seconds. Because Microsoft understands that you're working on a mobile device, which you might put aside at any moment, the Auto-Save feature is turned on by default. New documents are autosaved to the safest location, your iPad's internal storage, because it is inherently more reliable than a Wi-Fi connection to your OneDrive cloud storage.

After you have worked on a document for a while, you can check that it is automatically being saved to your iPad by tapping the File icon in the upper-left corner of the Ribbon (4.4). The File sheet shows that AutoSave is on and that changes are automatically being saved to your iPad (4.5).

▶ **NOTE** If you want, you can slide the AutoSave switch to Off, and a Save button will appear below the AutoSave control. From then on, with that document, you would need to save it manually. Given the benefits of automatically saving your document, I don't see why you would want to do that, but you can if you like.

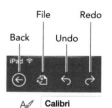

4.4 You'll do most of your file manipulation with the Back and File buttons in the Ribbon.

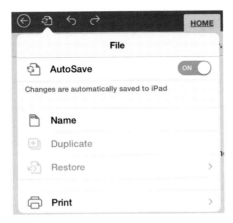

4.5 This File sheet shows that this particular document is being automatically saved to the iPad's internal storage.

Though the document is being autosaved to your iPad now, you may prefer that it instead be saved to your OneDrive cloud storage so you can access it on other devices, and in the process also give the document a name. Follow these steps:

1. Tap the File button on the Ribbon.

The File sheet appears, as shown in 4.5.

2. Tap Name.

The Save As dialog appears **(4.6)**.

4.6 By default, your OneDrive is selected as the default location for saving a document.

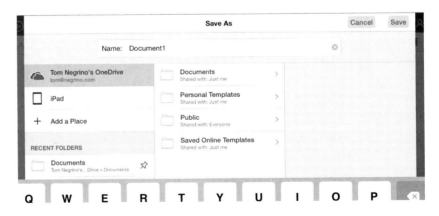

3. In the Name field, replace the default name with the name you want.

4. By default, the storage location for your document is your OneDrive; tap a OneDrive folder to choose where you want to store the document (4.7).

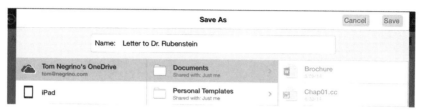

4.7 The Save As dialog gives you the chance to name the document, which will be saved in my OneDrive's Documents folder.

Note that you can also choose to continue saving the document to your iPad's internal storage by simply tapping iPad in the Save As dialog. Wherever you choose to save the document, to the cloud or local storage, that will become the location where the document is autosaved from then on.

5. Tap Save.

The file gets saved to your selected location, and you are returned to the document for further editing (4.8).

▶ **NOTE** Even though the file started out as being autosaved to your iPad's internal storage, once you save and name it, the file is moved to your selected storage location. If you save the file to your OneDrive, you won't find a vestigial copy of it in your iPad storage.

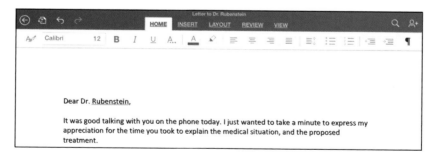

4.8 After the first time you save a document, Word assumes you want to continue working on it.

Opening Documents

When you launch one of the Office for iPad apps, it tries to help you get to work as soon as possible by opening to the Recent tab of the file manager (4.9). In the Recent tab, files are sorted and grouped chronologically.

4.9 The file manager's Recent view gives you a chronological retrospective of your work.

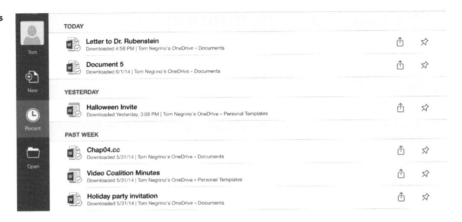

To open one of the documents on the Recent tab, simply tap on the document.

To open documents that aren't shown on the Recent tab, tap Open; then follow these steps:

1. In the first column, tap to select the storage location for the document: your OneDrive, your iPad's internal storage, or (if you're working in a business) a SharePoint server (4.10).

4.10 Tap to select your OneDrive as the location for the document. Your OneDrive's folders appear.

2. If you chose your OneDrive in Step 1, tap the folder that contains the document you're looking for; then tap to select and open the document you want.

or

If you chose iPad in Step 1, tap to select and open the document you want. (There are no folders in your iPad's internal storage.)

The document opens.

Refreshing Your Online Storage View

Your OneDrive storage is dynamic, and the contents of it may have changed since the last time you viewed it in the file manager of one of the Office for iPad apps. You can refresh the view from the server by tapping and dragging downwards on any of the columns in the file manager, which will refresh the view for that category in the file path. For example, if you want to refresh the folders on your OneDrive, tap and drag the folder column down (4.11). You see the standard "waiting" icon for a second at the top of the column; then the iPad will check with the OneDrive server, the view will refresh, and the column will return to normal.

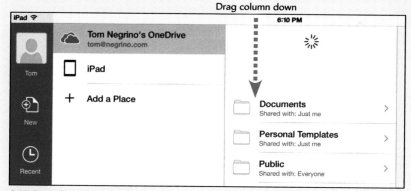

4.11 Drag down in a column to refresh the column's contents from the server.

That being said, I've experienced buggy behavior from the OneDrive system where I renamed a file on my Mac, OneDrive reported that the changes were synchronized, but the file didn't change its name on my Windows machine or iPad for hours. This may just be a bug that will be fixed soon, but you should occasionally make sure your file are changed as you expect.

Pinning documents

There's a way to keep frequently used documents available at the top of the Recent tab, ready for easy access: *pin* them. When you pin a document, a new Pinned section appears at the top of the Recent screen **(4.12)**.

Pinned icons

Share icons

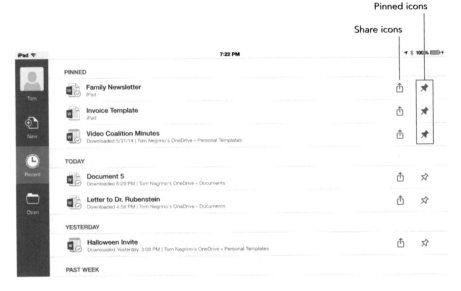

To pin or unpin a document, follow these steps:

1. In any of the Office for iPad apps, switch to the file manager.

2. If it isn't already set to the Recent tab, tap Recent.

3. Find the files that you want to pin to the top of the Recent list, and tap the pin icon to the right of their file names.

   A new Pinned section appears in the Recent list, with the file in it.

   or

   To unpin files and remove them from the Pinned section, tap the pin icon to the right of their filenames.

▶ **NOTE** Pinning a document only has an effect in the Recent list; it doesn't matter in the Open screen or in the OneDrive app.

Managing recent documents

The Recent list allows you to make some other changes to your files. Tapping the Share icon for a file in the Recent list displays a File sheet (4.13) with several functions:

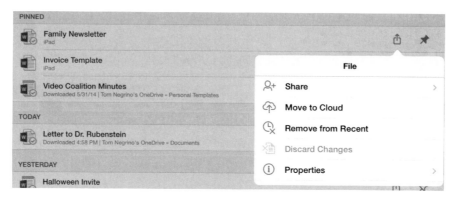

- **Share** is discussed in the next section.

- **Move to Cloud** is only active if the selected file resides in the iPad's internal storage. Tapping this command brings up a Choose Name and Location dialog that allows you to move the file to OneDrive.

- **Remove from Recent** removes the selected file from the Recent list, allowing you to declutter the list.

- **Discard Changes** is only active if you have turned autosave off for the document and allows you to abandon any changes you made to the document.

- **Properties** shows you additional information about the document (4.14).

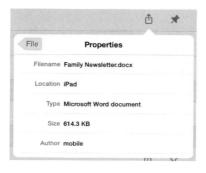

4.14 The Properties sheet gives you useful information about the document.

Sharing Documents

From any of the Office for iPad apps, you can share your documents with other people by tapping a Share icon in the Recent list of the file manager; from a Share icon in the Open list in the file manager; and from a Share icon in the Ribbon of the app (4.15).

4.15 Share icons are available to you in the Recent list (top); the Open list (middle); and in the document's Ribbon (bottom).

Tapping any of these Share icons allows you to share the document in one of three ways:

- **Email as Link** creates an email with a link to the document. You can choose to allow the recipient to View Only or View and Edit the document. Your file must be on OneDrive to use this option.

- **Email as Attachment** creates an email with the document as an attachment to the email. If the file is on your iPad, rather than on OneDrive, this is the only share option available to you.

- **Copy Link** is similar to Email as Link, except that it just gets a link and doesn't create an email. It's useful for when you want to include a link in a Web page or social media message. Your file must be on OneDrive to use this option.

To share a document, follow these steps:

1. Tap the Share icon.

   If you are in the Recent or Open list of the file manager, use the Share icons to the right of the file name. If you are editing a document, use the Share button at the right edge of the app's toolbar.

   The Share sheet appears (4.16).

Share icon

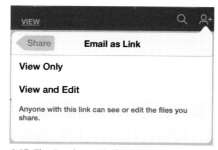

4.16 The Share sheet lets you share the document as an email or as a link.

4.17 The Email As Link sheet lets you choose whether the recipient will be able to only view or edit your document.

2. To share a link, tap either Email as Link or Copy Link.

   A second sheet appears, giving you the option to allow the recipient to either View Only or View and Edit the document (4.17).

3. Tap the option you want.

   If you are emailing the link, an email message appears, containing the link (4.18). Fill out the email message and send it on its way. If you chose to copy the link, the link is placed on the Clipboard, ready for you to switch to another app and paste it in.

   or

   If you chose to email the document as an attachment, an email message appears, with the document included (4.19). Address and send the message.

4.18 The email message contains the link to the shared document.

4.19 This email message contains the shared document as an attachment.

Printing Documents

To print from the iPad, you must have an AirPrint printer available on your network, or have software running on a Mac or other hardware that allows a printer to be seen as an AirPrint device. Follow these steps:

1. Open the document you want to print in one of the Office for iPad apps.

2. Tap the File icon; then tap Print (4.20).

   The Printer Options sheet appears (4.21).

3. Tap Select Printer.

   The Printer sheet appears, showing you the selection of printers on your network (4.22). In my case, I have software running on two devices that allow me different printing and virtual printing options.

4. Tap the printer you want to use.

   The Printer Options sheet reappears.

5. Make changes, if needed, for page range, the number of copies, and any printer options your printer may make available; then tap Print, which is now active.

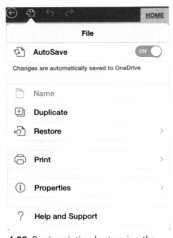

4.20 Begin printing by tapping the File icon in the Ribbon.

4.21 You need to select your printer from the Printer Options sheet.

4.22 Choose your printer from the displayed options.

Introducing the Office for iPad Interface

The interfaces of all the Office for iPad apps are intentionally similar to recent desktop versions of Microsoft Office. As befits the iPad, the apps have been pared down to better use the touch interface, but they still have the Ribbon, the toolbar at the top of the screen, split into tabs that logically group together the different functions of the app (4.23). Each tab has controls that make sense for it; for example, the Home tab in each app contains a toolbar with the most-often-used controls, as determined by many thousands of hours of user-interface research. Tap the name of a tab to display the tools related to the task at hand. When certain objects are selected in a document, contextual tabs appear, offering controls and options related to that object (which could be a table, an image, a chart, or other document elements). If you need a little more room on the page, tap a tab name, which hides or shows its controls.

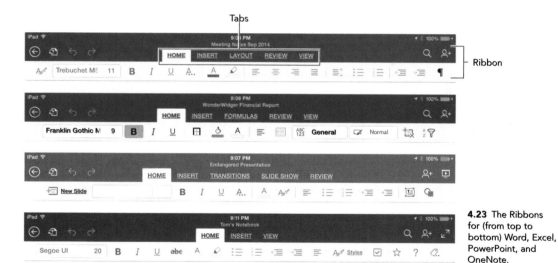

4.23 The Ribbons for (from top to bottom) Word, Excel, PowerPoint, and OneNote.

Some controls on the Ribbon have options that appear in a sheet when you tap the control (4.24). But Microsoft has actually done a better job with adapting the Office apps for iPad than it has adapting them for Windows tablets, which still have user interface elements more suited to mice and keyboards, such as dialog boxes.

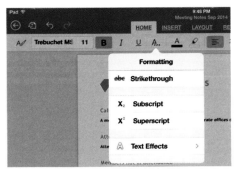

4.24 Some Ribbon controls have additional options.

4.25 You can use Word in portrait (shown here) or landscape mode, and you can zoom the document as you like.

At the left side of the Ribbon in all the apps, you'll find four buttons (4.4): Back, which brings you to the file manager; File, which displays the File sheet discussed earlier in this chapter; and the Undo and Redo buttons. On the right edge of the Ribbon is a Share icon allowing you to share the document and a Find icon allowing you to search the document. (Power-Point lacks this button.)

Below the Ribbon is a document area. All of the apps conform to the standard iPad method of resizing your document view. Just pinch and spread your fingers to zoom the document as needed (4.25). All the apps except for PowerPoint work in either landscape or portrait mode; PowerPoint only works in landscape orientation.

CHAPTER 5

Working with Templates

With an Office 365 subscription, you can use the Office for iPad apps to create documents. Of course, you can always create documents from scratch, using a blank canvas (see Chapter 4), but Microsoft makes between 14 and 20 templates available to you inside the Word, Excel, and PowerPoint apps. A *template* is a premade document that serves as a starting point for your own document. It usually contains *placeholder* information that you replace with your own content. By using templates, you get nicely designed documents without having to learn the (often tedious) process of how to make them pretty by yourself. But templates are important for other reasons on the iPad: because of the inherent limitations of the device, the software, and...well, *you.*

The iPad has a limited screen size, and your built-in pointing device—your finger—is much less precise than a mouse pointer. Besides that, Microsoft has wisely not attempted to cram in every feature from the desktop Office apps to the iPad versions, so to get the most work done in the mobile environment, you should take advantage of other people's work and start off your own documents from a template whenever you can. You'll get more and better work done.

You also have access to other versions of Microsoft Office as part of your Office 365 subscription, and additional templates are available from the desktop and browser-based versions of Office. These templates are available to you online; you can easily save them to your OneDrive and then continue work on the iPad.

In this chapter, you see how to create new documents from the built-in document templates; bring templates in from the desktop versions of Office; and access and save the online templates.

Creating Documents from the Built-In Templates

You create documents with three of the four Office for iPad apps: Word, Excel, and PowerPoint. The fourth app, OneNote, technically has one document (called a *notebook)* into which you put all your information. (It's certainly possible to have multiple notebooks in OneNote, but that's a technique that's used almost entirely by advanced users.)

Word, Excel, and PowerPoint each have a relatively small number of built-in templates to get you started, and you access them in the same way in each app. Follow these steps:

1. On the iPad, tap the icon for the app you want to use (5.1).

    In this example, start with Excel.

    The app starts, set to the Open tab (5.2). By default, the file manager is set to your OneDrive cloud account, showing you the folders inside your OneDrive folder.

5.1 On your iPad, tap the app you want to use.

5.2 For safety's sake and automatic backup, documents are automatically saved to your OneDrive cloud storage, which is selected by default.

2. Tap the New icon on the left side of the screen.

The screen changes to show you the app's selection of previews of the built-in templates (5.3). The first template, in the upper-left position, is always a blank document, whether it be a blank word processing document for Word, a blank worksheet for Excel, or a blank presentation for PowerPoint.

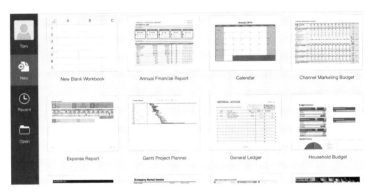

5.3 Tapping the New icon shows you the small selection of built-in templates.

3. If necessary, scroll through the built-in templates until you find one you want; then tap the preview icon.

The template opens (5.4).

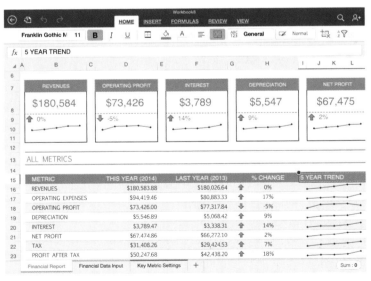

5.4 Tapping a template creates a new document based on that template, usually with sample text or data included.

▶ **TIP** Many of the templates have instruction balloons to help you use them better (5.5), and some of the Excel templates consist of multiple worksheets combined into a single workbook.

5.5 You can zoom out of the document by touching the screen and spreading your fingers, which shows the template's instruction balloons.

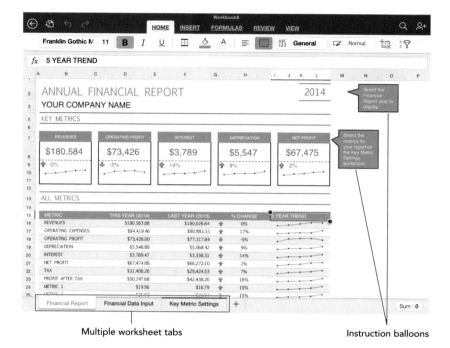

Multiple worksheet tabs   Instruction balloons

4. Replace the placeholder information in the template with your own work.

5. Name and save your document.

   Since it was created from a template, your document doesn't yet have a name (though it has actually been autosaving to your local iPad storage every few seconds). There are two slightly different ways to name and save your document where you want to save it:

   Back   File

   5.6 You start naming and saving a document by tapping either the Back or File icon.

   • The first method, and my preferred one, is to tap the Back button at the top-left corner of the screen (5.6). That brings up the Save As dialog (5.7), allowing you to enter the name of your document in the Name field, as well as choose the location for where you want to save it on either your OneDrive or your iPad's internal storage. The reason I prefer this method is because when you do it this way the Save As dialog includes a Delete button, in case you want to abandon your work altogether. It just gives you a little more flexibility, and saves you a step over the next method.

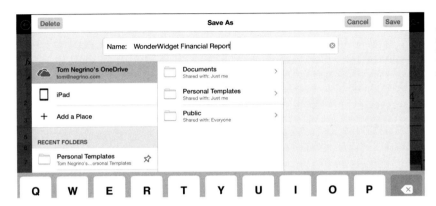

5.7 In the Save As dialog, you can enter a name for the document and choose where you want to save it.

- The other method to save your document and give it a name is to tap the File button at the top-left corner of the screen, which brings up the File popover (5.8). In this popover, tap Name, which also brings up the Save As dialog (though missing the Delete button). You can then enter the name for your document and choose where you want to save it.

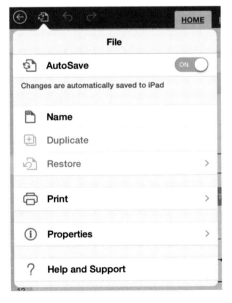

5.8 Tapping the File icon brings up the File popover, which also allows you to name the document.

6. After naming the document using either method, tap the Save button.

   The app assumes that you are done with the document for now and returns you to the file manager, set to the Recent tab (5.9). You see the document you just saved at the top of the list.

5.9 Back in the file manager's Recent tab, the file you just finished working on is at the top of the list.

Importing Templates from Desktop Versions of Office

Microsoft Office has been around for a very long time for both Windows and Mac (though it's a little-known historical fact that the Mac version appeared in 1989, more than a year before the Windows version). For most of that time, Microsoft has provided Office users with many premade templates for the various Office applications. This vast template library, consisting of thousands of different template files, is available to the desktop versions of Office. You can't access that template library directly from the iPad versions of Office, but because the desktop versions are included in your Office 365 subscription, you can use the Windows or Mac versions to download templates, which you can then easily transfer to the iPad via OneDrive. The process requires a little bit of a workaround to make sure you will end up with the right kinds of files on your iPad, but once you understand how to do it, you vastly increase the template choices available to the iPad apps.

Understanding the Template Libraries

As I mention back in Chapter 1, the Microsoft Office file formats have changed over the years, and Microsoft has created several different template libraries, some of which use the current file formats and some of which use older file formats. The Office for iPad apps' native Office file formats are the modern XML-based document formats (.docx, .xlsx, and .pptx). The main Office Templates site, which for the United States is http://office.microsoft.com/en-us/templates, identifies four separate template libraries:

- Templates for Office Online are premade templates meant for use with the free, browser-based version of the Office apps. These templates are in a file format that is compatible with the Office for iPad apps.

- Templates for Office 2013 for Windows are built directly into the New dialog in the Office 2013 programs. They are based online and require a connection to the Internet. These templates are also in a modern file format that is compatible with the Office for iPad apps.

- Templates for Office 2010 for Windows are templates that were installed onto the local PC when Microsoft Office was installed, with the ability to access additional online templates. This hybrid partially local/partially online approach is shared by Microsoft Office 2011 for the Mac, and it appears that the Mac version shares the Office 2010 for Windows online templates. These templates use the modern XML-based file formats, though many Mac users in particular inexplicably still save files in the older formats (.doc, .xls, .ppt), which should be avoided for use with the iPad.

- Templates for Microsoft Word 2007 for Windows were installed on local machines and of course used older file formats. Because of the age of the suite, I won't discuss how to use those templates.

Importing templates from Office 2013 in Windows

If you have downloaded and installed Office 2013 for Windows as part of your Office 365 subscription, you'll find it especially easy to access its templates and get them on your iPad. The different Office programs have literally thousands of templates available, all in file formats compatible with

Office for iPad. First, you need to find a template; then you need to save it to your OneDrive as a template, not as a regular document, so that Office for iPad will always be able to use the file as a jumping-off point.

One issue you may have to deal with is that fonts used in document templates may not be available on the iPad, but I deal more with that subject in Chapter 8. Follow these steps:

1. In one of the Office 2013 for Windows programs (I use Word as an example here), click the File tab **(5.10)**.

   This brings you to a view that Microsoft calls the Backstage **(5.11)**. The Backstage is where you perform file management like saving, sharing, and exporting documents, and printing.

5.10 In Word 2013 for Windows, begin searching for templates by clicking the File tab.

5.11 You use Word 2013's new Backstage view for file management tasks, including searching for templates for new documents.

2. Click New.

3. Chances are the template you want won't be displayed by default, so type a description in the Backstage's search field and press Enter, or click one of the Suggested Searches links below the search field **(5.12)**.

5.12 Type one or more keywords into the search field to try to find an appropriate template.

Many different templates based on your search appear **(5.13)**. If you like, you may filter the search results further by clicking one or more of the category links on the right side of the window.

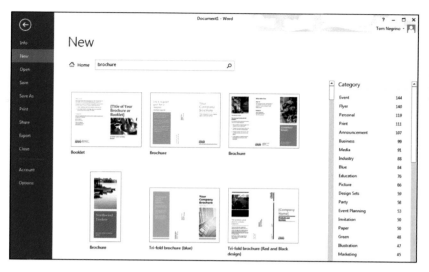

5.13 If you are overwhelmed with the number of search results, you can filter them by clicking one or more of the categories in the list on the right.

4. When you find the template you want, double-click it to open it **(5.14)**.

As usual when starting from a template, the document is opened as an untitled document. What you need to do to make it available for use on Office for iPad is save it to your OneDrive in the template format, not in the document format.

5.14 Double-clicking a template in the Backstage opens it in Word.

5. Click the File tab; then, when the Backstage appears, click Save As.

   You get the option of saving the file on your OneDrive or on your computer (5.15). Make sure that OneDrive is selected, which shows you recent folders you've accessed on your OneDrive, plus a Browse button that shows you the entire contents of your OneDrive.

6. Click Browse.

   The Save As dialog appears (5.16). In this dialog, you need to do four things. First, in the File Name field, give the template file a name. Second, from the Save As Type pop-up menu, you must choose Word Template. This gives the file the necessary .dotx file extension so that Word for iPad will recognize the file as a template, not as a regular document. Making the file a template will also automatically switch the Save As location to the location set in Word's Settings for templates, which isn't what you want. So third, navigate back to your OneDrive folder (the easiest way to do that is to click the Back button in the Save As dialog) and decide where you want to put your template files. (I created a folder in my OneDrive called Personal Templates.) Finally, click the Save button to save the new template in your OneDrive folder.

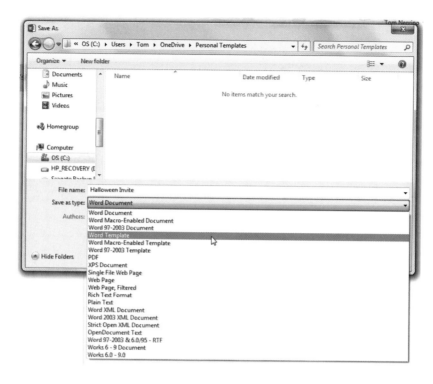

5.16 In the Save As dialog, name your template, save it to your OneDrive, and make sure you save it in the Word Template format.

7. To use the new template on your iPad, open the appropriate app for the template; choose Open in the file manager; navigate to where you saved the template (5.17); and then tap the template.

   The file opens as a new untitled document in the iPad app (5.18).

5.17 In Word for iPad's file manager, the new template appears in my Personal Templates folder.

5.18 Tapping the template file opens a new untitled document in Word for iPad.

Importing templates from Office 2011 for Mac

Office 2011 for Mac, which is available as part of the Office 365 subscription, comes with hundreds of templates, some installed on your Mac and others available online. No matter which template you choose, you need to first open it on your Mac and then save it onto your OneDrive as a template file, not as a document file, so the corresponding iPad app will be able to use a template to create new documents. Follow these steps:

1. In one of the Office 2011 for Mac programs (I use Word as an example because it has the largest variety of templates), choose File > New from Template.

    The Document Gallery appears (5.19).

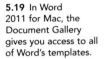

5.19 In Word 2011 for Mac, the Document Gallery gives you access to all of Word's templates.

2. From the Templates categories in the left pane, or from the Online Templates portion at the bottom of that pane, choose the category; then select the template you want to use by clicking it.

3. (Optional) Some Word templates allow you to customize the color and font schemes for the document in the right preview pane, so set these if you like.

4. Click Choose.

The template opens as an untitled document (5.20).

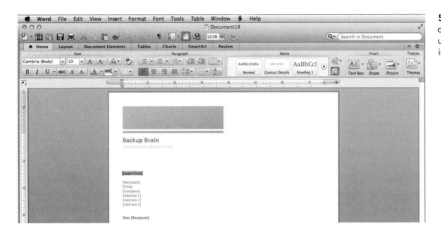

5.20 The template opens as a new untitled document in Word.

5. To save the document so it can be accessed as a template from Office for iPad, choose File > Save As.

The Save As dialog appears (5.21).

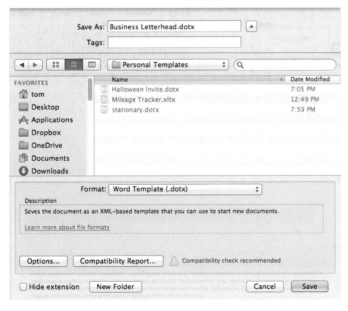

5.21 In the Mac's Save As dialog, you need to give the new template a name, specify where you want to save it on your OneDrive, and save it in the Word Template format.

6. In this dialog, do the following.

First, in the Save As field, give the template file a name. Second, from the Format pop-up menu, choose Word Template (.dotx). This gives the file the necessary .dotx file extension so that Word for iPad will recognize the file as a template, not as a regular document. Unfortunately, it also automatically switches your Save As dialog's location to your My Templates folder on your Mac. That isn't where you want to save the file, so navigate back to your OneDrive folder and choose where you want to put your template file. (I created a folder in my OneDrive folder called Personal Templates.) Finally, click the Save button to save the new template in your OneDrive folder.

7. To use the new template on your iPad, open the appropriate app for the template; choose Open in the file manager; navigate to where you saved the template; and then tap the template.

The file opens as a new untitled document in the iPad app (5.22).

▶ **TIP** Some placeholder text in the document may not look exactly the same on the Mac and on the iPad, because that placeholder information relies on information from the respective device's Contacts. If the contact information isn't the same on both devices, you may get a default placeholder on one device or the other. (Compare the organization names in 5.20 and 5.22 for an example.)

5.22 Opening the template from your OneDrive on Word for iPad gives you a new untitled document.

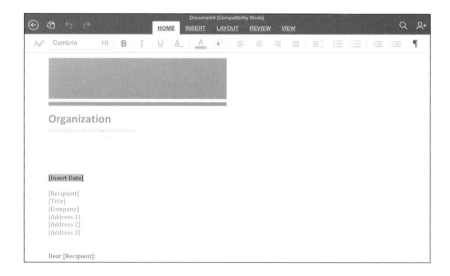

Importing Templates
from Office Online

Office Online is the limited versions of the Office apps that you can use online with nothing more than a browser and that are free to use by all. I cover Office Online in much more detail in Chapter 7, but what I'm interested in here is the extensive selection of Word, Excel, and PowerPoint templates that are available to the Office Online user and that can be saved for use on your iPad. These are a different set of templates from those available in other versions of Office.

Since Office Online doesn't give you the control over saving items in the same way the Office desktop version do, you can use two different techniques to save and use the Office Online templates. I run through them both in this section.

Duplicating saved documents

In this first technique, all you need are the Office Online Web app and its corresponding Office for iPad app, and you need to always duplicate your "template" file as soon as you open it. (The reason for the quotes around "template" will soon become clear.) Follow these steps:

1. Start with Office Online by going to https://office.com in any Web browser (5.23).

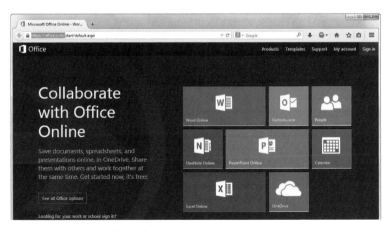

5.23 You can use any modern browser to access Office Online. In this case, I'm using Firefox for Windows.

2. Click to choose the application you want to use.

   In this example, use PowerPoint Online.

3. In the Let's Get Started screen, click the Browse Templates button **(5.24)**.

5.24 Click the Browse Templates button to access the Office Online templates.

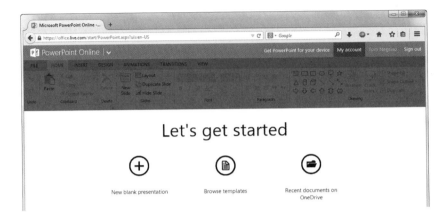

4. On the next screen, choose the template you want to use **(5.25)**.

   You can click one of the links below Browse by Category to narrow your choices.

5.25 Find and select the template you want.

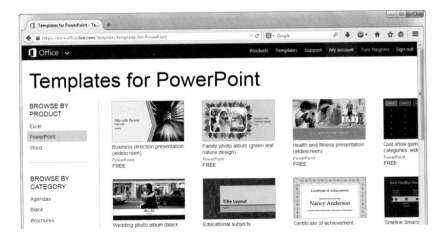

The template's detail screen gives you more information about the template and a larger thumbnail picture of it.

5. Click the Open in [*App Name*] Online button (**5.26**).

You're warned that your document will be saved to your OneDrive (**5.27**).

5.26 When you're sure the template is what you want, click the Open button.

5.27 Click Continue on this annoying and time-wasting screen.

6. Click Continue (5.27).

The document opens, ready for editing in the browser (**5.28**). As you can see from the bar at the top of the screen, the file is being automatically saved in your OneDrive/Documents folder, and it has a default name (such as Presentation for a PowerPoint document or Document for a Word document). You can't change the document path from inside Office Online, but you can change the default name of the document.

Document path   Document name

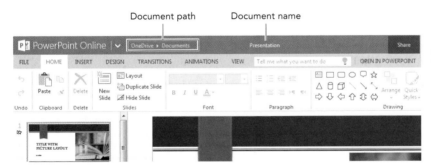

5.28 When your document opens in the Office Online app, it's automatically saved to your OneDrive and given a default name.

7. In the top bar of the document, click the name of the document to edit it, and give it a name that will remind you that you mean to use it as a template (**5.29**).

5.29 Give the document name that will help you use it as a template.

You have to do this because the Office Online programs can't actually save in the actual template formats; they can only save in the document formats. As soon as you give the document its new name, it is automatically saved again.

8. Close the browser window with the Office Online document.

Now would be a good time to read the "Organizing Your Templates" sidebar later in this section.

9. On the iPad, open the app that corresponds to the document you were just working with on Office Online.

You may need to use the Open tab in the app's file manager, and you'll find the document you want inside your OneDrive's Documents folder (5.30).

Document from Office Online

5.30 On the iPad, you'll originally find the document in your Documents folder.

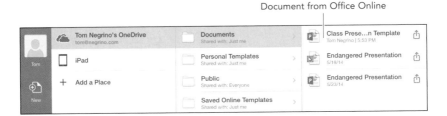

10. Tap the document to open it.

Organizing Your Templates

I like to save my templates in a place where they will be easily grouped, recognized, and used, so I created a folder in my OneDrive (refer to 5.30) named Saved Online Templates. You can create that folder in your OneDrive folder on either your Mac or Windows desktop, or you can use the OneDrive app on your iPad. I also have a different templates folder in my OneDrive called Personal Templates, which contains actual template files, instead of the Office Online documents that I need to duplicate to use as templates. That method of organization works for me, but you may prefer something entirely different. There's no right way to do it; it's whatever works best for you.

11. After the document is open, tap the File icon at the top of the screen and choose Duplicate from the popover (5.31).

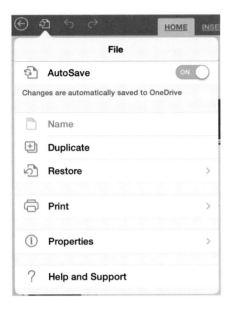

5.31 In the Office for iPad app, tap the File icon and choose Duplicate.

12. In the resulting Choose Name and Location screen, choose the location on your OneDrive for the duplicated file and also select the OneDrive folder where you want the file to be saved (5.32).

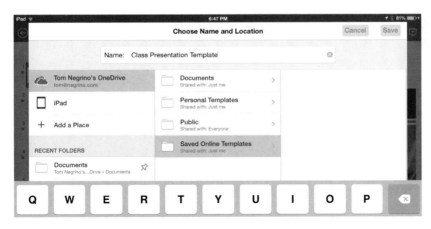

5.32 In the Choose Name and Location dialog, choose where you want to save your new template.

13. Tap Save to save the document in your chosen location.

14. When you want to reuse the file as a template, open it from the Office for iPad's file manager; immediately repeat Steps 11–13 to save it in a different location, and then make changes as you would with any template-based file.

Saving Office Online templates with the desktop versions of Office

If you have installed the desktop versions of Microsoft office for either Windows or Mac, you can open Office Online templates in a desktop version of the app and then save the file as a real template file, using the native Office template formats. For this example, I use Word 2013 for Windows as the example program, but the process is similar for any of the Office apps on either of the desktop platforms. Follow these steps:

1. Start with Office Online by going to https://office.com in any Web browser.

2. Click to choose the application you want to use.

3. On the Let's Get Started screen, click the Browse Templates button.

4. On the next screen, choose the template you want to use.

The template's detail screen gives you more information about the template and a larger thumbnail picture of it.

5. Click the Open in [*App Name*] Online button.

You're warned that your document will be saved to your OneDrive.

6. Click Continue.

The document opens, ready for editing in the browser (**5.33**).

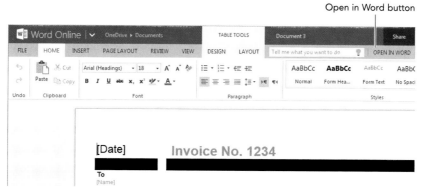

Open in Word button

5.33 Begin creating a new template by opening one of the Online templates in one of the Office Online Web apps.

7. Rather than continue to edit in Word Online, move the document into Word 2013 by clicking the Open in Word button.

Depending on how your system is configured, you may get a dialog asking for permission to open the desktop version of Word on your machine (**5.34**).

5.34 For security reasons, your system will probably ask you if it's really okay to open the current Web document in the desktop version of Office.

This dialog will look different depending on the browser you're using, on whether you're using a Windows PC or Mac, and perhaps on whether you have multiple versions of Microsoft Word on your machine.

8. Click OK (or whatever the button that grants permission for Word to open is called).

The file opens in Word.

9. Save the open document as a Word template (5.35).

Use the procedure in "Importing templates from Office 2013 in Windows" earlier in this chapter.

5.35 Once the online template is opened in the desktop version of your Office app, save it as a template.

CHAPTER 6

Using the OneDrive App

Most of the time, you'll be doing your work in one of the Office for iPad apps. But one iOS app in the suite—the OneDrive app—allows you to view and manage the folders and documents on your OneDrive. And unlike the other apps, it doesn't only run on the iPad; it also works on the iPhone and iPod touch, so you can use those smaller-screened devices to work with your files.

In this chapter, you see how you can use the OneDrive app to create new OneDrive folders; rename and delete folders and files; view documents; and work with Recent and Shared documents.

Introducing the OneDrive App

The OneDrive app is meant to help you easily work with folders and files in your OneDrive cloud storage. The app gives you a view inside your OneDrive cloud storage, along with tools for selecting and manipulating the contents of the storage.

Some of the things you can do with the OneDrive app you can also do inside your OneDrive folder for Mac or Windows. For example, you can add, delete, and rename folders on the Mac or Windows desktops (and, in fact, probably do it easier than by using the app). But the app allows you to do these things without leaving the iOS environment and while you are on the go. You can also do a few things with the OneDrive app you can't do on the computer desktop, such as get a view of and work with Recent or Shared files and folders.

Signing in to the OneDrive app

When you launch the OneDrive app, you'll be asked to log into your OneDrive account (a.k.a. your Microsoft account). This login uses the same username and password as the rest of your Office 365 subscription, but logging in to the OneDrive app isn't connected to the rest of the Office apps in the suite. For example, if you log in to Word for iPad with your Microsoft account, you will also have logged in to Excel, PowerPoint, and OneNote on the device. But you'll still need to log in to the OneDrive app separately.

To log in to the OneDrive app, follow these steps:

1. Find and tap the OneDrive app's icon.

2. On the welcome screen, tap Sign In (6.1).

3. On the Sign In screen, enter your username and the password for your Microsoft account; then tap Sign In (6.2).

OneDrive

Sign In

Sign into OneDrive using your Microsoft
account. This should be the same
account that you use to access other
Microsoft services like Outlook.com,
Xbox Live, or MSN.

6.1 Tap the Sign in button on the
welcome screen to get started.

❮ Back   **OneDrive**

Sign in

Microsoft account

Password
••••••••

Sign in

6.2 Type your Microsoft account
credentials.

4. (Optional) On the next screen, which invites you to turn on Camera
   Backup, tap OK or No Thanks (6.3).

   Camera Backup automatically uploads photos you take with this particular device to OneDrive. If you turn on this feature, Microsoft awards
   you another free 3 GB of storage, though that 3 GB is added to your
   OneDrive account, not per device. So if you turn on Camera Backup
   on more than one device, you still only gain an extra 3 GB of storage.

Your photos, always with you

Turn on Camera Backup to
automatically upload your
photos to OneDrive. You'll get
3 GB of additional storage for
free.

OK

No thanks

6.3 If you want the
contents of your
Camera Roll to
be automatically
uploaded and backed
up to your OneDrive,
tap OK.

If you choose not to turn on Camera Backup at this time, you still have
the opportunity to turn it on later, using the OneDrive app's Settings. Also, you see this screen, asking you to enable Camera Backup,
only once.

After you make your choice, the folders in your OneDrive storage appear (6.4).

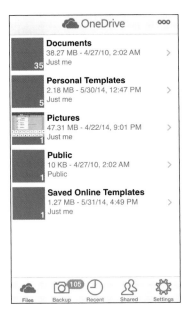

6.4 After you sign in, you see the folders at the top level of your OneDrive.

Touring the OneDrive app

The OneDrive app screen is split into three areas (6.5). At the top of the screen is the *toolbar*, which is context-sensitive; the contents of the toolbar change depending on what you are doing with the app. At the right end of the toolbar you find the Actions button, which allows you to manipulate items. As you see later in this chapter, sometimes the toolbar can migrate down to the bottom of the screen, replacing the Tab bar.

The main part of the screen is taken up by the *Items area*, which is where you see folders (represented as square icons) and (when you're viewing the contents of a folder) document icons. Each folder shows you its name, the size of its contents, its creation date and time, and with whom it is shared.

At the bottom of the screen is the *Tab bar*. Most of the time you'll be working in the Files tab, but there are other tabs for Camera Backup, Recent files, and Shared files. At the right end of the Tab bar is the Settings button, which I discuss in "Using Settings" later in this chapter.

Toolbar   Folder   Actions

6.5 The home view of
the OneDrive app on
the iPad.

Items area   Tab bar   Settings

Working with Folders

When working with files and folders on the Mac or Windows desktops,
you're used to directly manipulating the objects with which you're working. For example, you can drag a file or folder to the Trash or Recycle Bin
to delete it, or drag one folder into another. You can't do that sort of thing
in iOS, so you usually have to resort to multiple steps. First, you need to
enter a selection mode; next, you select the item you want to change;
then you make the change you want. It's a little more cumbersome than
direct manipulation of objects, but it's what needed in the current state
of the iOS art.

Creating folders

In this example, you create a new folder at the top level of your OneDrive storage. Before you start, things may look like (6.6) on the Mac desktop and like (6.7) in the OneDrive app.

6.6 Before you create a folder, this is what OneDrive might look like on the Mac.

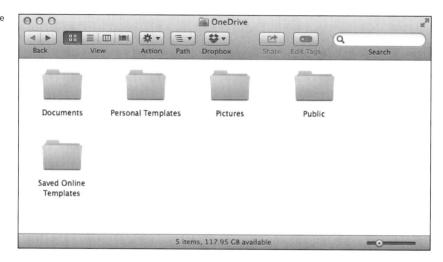

6.7 The OneDrive app shows folders differently from Mac and Windows.

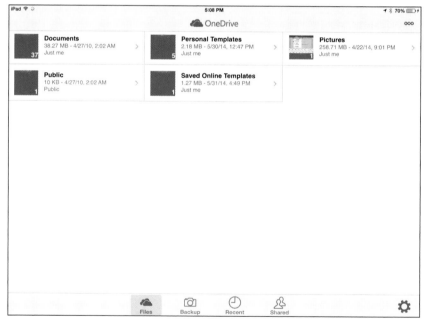

To create a new folder at the top level of the OneDrive folder, follow these steps:

1. Tap the Actions button at the upper right of the screen.

   A sheet appears with your choices (6.8).

   6.8 Begin adding a folder by tapping the Actions button near the top of the screen.

2. Tap Add Items.

   The sheet changes to show the next level of choices (6.9).

   6.9 When you have chosen to add items, this sheet shows additional options.

3. Tap Create a Folder.

   The Create a Folder sheet appears.

   ▶ **TIP** There is no Cancel button in the Create a Folder sheet, but if you choose not to continue with the process, just tap anywhere else on the screen away from the sheet. The sheet disappears and the process is canceled.

4. Backspace over the default name in the Folder Name field, type your desired folder name, and then tap Create (6.10).

   6.10 Enter a name for the new folder in the Folder Name field.

The OneDrive app creates the folder and assumes you'll be working further inside the folder, so it switches the view to show the new folder's contents (6.11). Notice that the context-sensitive toolbar has changed; the title shows you the name of the folder you are in, and a new Files button appears to bring you back a level.

Back
one level

Folder title

6.11 After folder creation, you stay in the new folder for additional work.

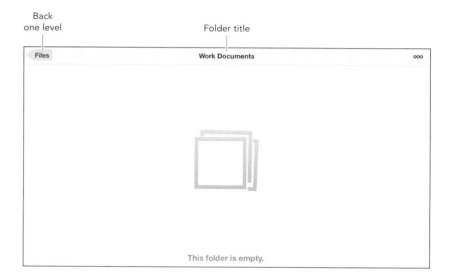

Files   **Work Documents**   ooo

This folder is empty.

5. Tap the Files button to return to the top level of your OneDrive storage.

You can see your new folder in both iOS and on the computer desktop (6.12).

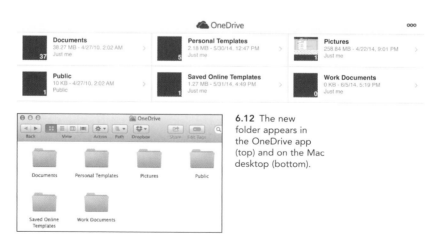

OneDrive   ooo

Documents
38.27 MB - 4/27/10, 2:02 AM
Just me

Personal Templates
2.18 MB - 5/30/14, 12:47 PM
Just me

Pictures
258.84 MB - 4/22/14, 9:01 PM
Just me

Public
10 KB - 4/27/10, 2:02 AM
Public

Saved Online Templates
1.27 MB - 5/31/14, 4:49 PM
Just me

Work Documents
0 KB - 6/5/14, 5:19 PM
Just me

6.12 The new folder appears in the OneDrive app (top) and on the Mac desktop (bottom).

Renaming folders

There are two ways to rename a folder. If you are inside the folder, you can rename it directly. But if you are not viewing the contents of the folder, you first need to select the folder and then work through the renaming process.

Follow these steps if you are currently inside a folder:

1. Tap the Actions button.

   A sheet appears with the possible actions you can take for the folder (6.13).

6.13 Tapping the Actions button shows you your possible actions.

2. Tap Rename This Folder.

   The Rename sheet appears.

3. Change the folder name in the Name field (6.14); then tap Done.

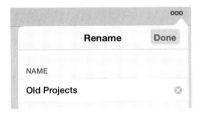

6.14 Type the new name of the folder in the Name field of the Rename sheet.

If you are not currently viewing the contents of a folder that you want to rename, follow these steps:

1. In the OneDrive app, navigate so you can see the icon for the folder.

2. Tap the Actions button.

   A sheet appears with the possible actions you can take for the folder
   (6.15). Note that the Actions sheet is context-sensitive, so it doesn't
   look the same as the sheet in 6.13.

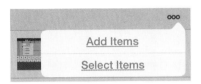

6.15 The Actions
sheet is contextsensi-
tive, so it changes
depending on what
you are doing.

3. Tap Select Items.

   The screen changes to the Select Items screen, with three important
   changes. First, the Actions button has been replaced with a Cancel
   button. Second, selection circles appear next to each of the items in
   the Items area. Last, the toolbar has migrated down to the bottom
   of the screen and will become active once you select one or more
   items (6.16).

Selection circles

6.16 You can pick
one or more items
in the Select Items
screen.

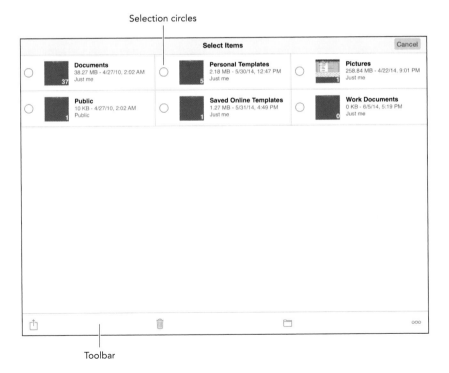

Toolbar

4. Tap the selection circle next to the folder you want to rename.

   You can rename only one folder at a time.

5. Tap the Actions button, which is now in the toolbar at the bottom of the screen.

   A sheet appears with context-appropriate actions (6.17).

6.17 To rename the folder, use the Actions button at the bottom of the screen.

6. Tap Rename This Folder.

   The Rename sheet appears (refer to 6.14).

7. Change the folder name in the Name field; then tap Done.

   The name of the folder changes, and the OneDrive app keeps you in selection mode, in case you want to make other changes.

8. If you are done making changes, tap Cancel to exit selection mode.

Deleting and moving folders

Deleting and moving folders is similar to renaming them. First, you must select the folder or folders; then you perform an action upon the selection. Follow these steps:

1. In the OneDrive app, navigate so you can see the icon for the folder.

2. Tap the Actions button.

   A sheet appears with the possible actions you can take for the folder (refer to 6.15).

3. Tap Select Items.

   The screen changes to the Select Items screen.

4. Tap the selection circle next to the item you want to change (6.18).

   You may select multiple items. When you do, the title at the top of the screen tells you how many items are selected. Selecting items also activates the Delete and Move icons in the toolbar at the bottom of the screen.

6.18 For some actions, you may select multiple items.

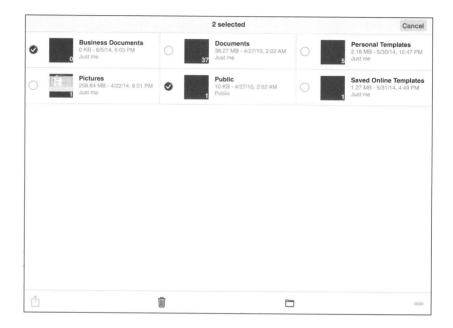

5. To delete the selected items, tap the Delete icon in the toolbar.

   The OneDrive app shows a dialog asking you to confirm your choice. Tap OK and can skip the rest of the steps in this section. You can retrieve items that you accidentally delete by going to the Recycle Bin via the Web interface at https://onedrive.com.

6. To move the selected items, tap the Move icon in the toolbar.

   The Files sheet appears, showing other folders on your OneDrive (6.19).

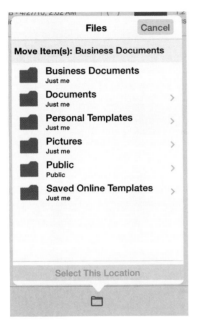

6.19 You can use the Files sheet to navigate the folders on your OneDrive.

7. Tap the icon of the folder where you want to move the selected item.

   The view in the File sheet changes as you navigate.

8. When you reach the correct location, tap Select This Location.

   The OneDrive app moves the selected item.

Working with Files

The OneDrive app has a built-in file viewer for Microsoft Office documents and for other common file formats that can be read by iOS, including graphics files (in JPEG, PNG, TIF, and GIF formats), and PDF files, among other formats. You can also use the OneDrive file viewer to open Office documents for editing in the Office for iPad apps and, in many cases, to open other files for editing in other apps you may have on your iPad.

Please Stand By

One quirk you should know about the OneDrive app is that whenever you work with a file—whether it be viewing the file in the built-in file viewer or opening the file in another app on your iPad—the OneDrive app always downloads the file to your iPad before it performs the action. Most of the time, this isn't a big deal, because many files, such as Word and Excel documents, aren't that big and don't take very long to download over Wi-Fi. But if you're dealing with an image file, PowerPoint presentation, or a PDF that is more than 1 MB or so, there may be a noticeable delay before the OneDrive app is ready to perform its action. While the download is happening, you always get a little progress box to give you an idea of how long it will be until you can continue your work.

If the file has been recently downloaded and cached, the OneDrive app checks to make sure it is unchanged from the server version, and if it has not, it uses the already local version to save you time and bandwidth.

Viewing and opening Office files

Opening Office files from the OneDrive app is easy. Follow these steps:

1. Navigate to the Office file you want to view (6.20).

2. Tap the file in the Items list.

   The file opens in the built-in file viewer (6.21).

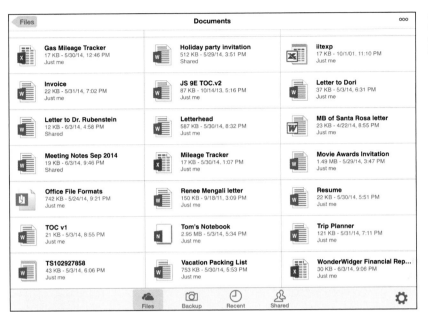

6.20 In the Files view, Office documents show their familiar icons.

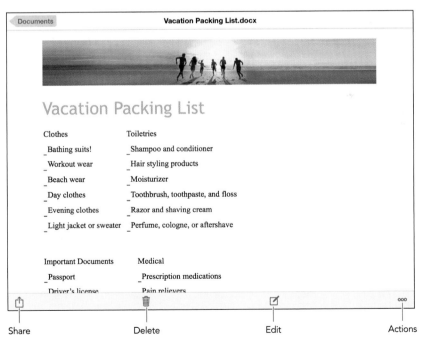

6.21 In the OneDrive app's file viewer, you get a quick-and-dirty view of the file.

The OneDrive file viewer isn't designed to show the files with complete and correct fidelity; it's mainly there to give you a reasonable preview of the document. That's why in 6.21, the fonts are different from what they look like in Word. There is a toolbar at the bottom of the file viewer screen that disappears after a second so you get as tall a preview of the document as possible.

3. If the toolbar has disappeared, tap the middle of the screen to redisplay it; then tap the Edit button.

The document opens in the appropriate Office for iPad app (6.22). Note that the document appears in a full-fidelity view in the Office app.

6.22 In Word for IPad, fonts and the lines before each item appear correctly.

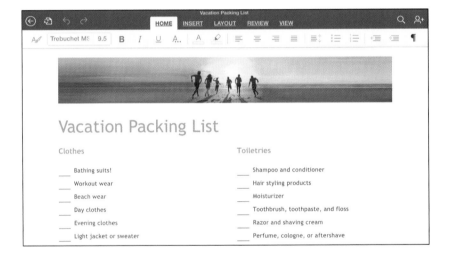

Viewing and opening other files

You can also open some, but not all, files in your OneDrive in other apps that may be on your iPad. The reason why this might not work is complicated, but it has to do with Apple's security model for the iPad and whether third-party developers have written their apps in such a way that OneDrive can recognize them as file viewers/editors for a given file. To (if possible) view and open non-Office files, follow these steps:

1. Navigate to the non-Office file you want to view.

2. Tap the file in the Items list.

The file opens in the built-in file viewer. Again, depending on the file, it may not look perfect; that's because of issues with the OneDrive file viewer, not the file itself.

If the file can't be viewed at all, OneDrive shows you whatever information it can about the file (6.23).

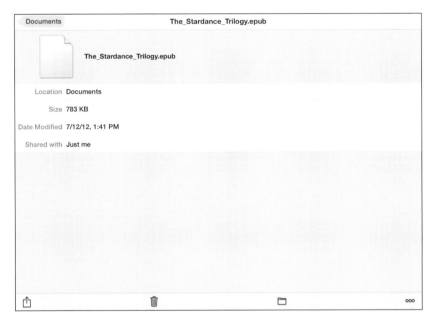

6.23 When the OneDrive app's file viewer can't read the file, it shows you this informational screen.

3. Tap the Actions button in the toolbar.

    If the toolbar has disappeared, tap the middle of the screen to redisplay it. A context-appropriate sheet appears with the available actions (6.24).

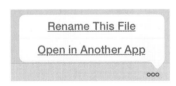

6.24 Because the OneDrive app can't do anything else with this file, it offers to let you rename it or open it in another app.

4. Tap Open in Another App.

    The file open sheet appears, showing you a horizontally scrolling list of apps that might be able to open the file.

5. Swipe to scroll the list until you find the most likely app; then tap its icon (6.25).

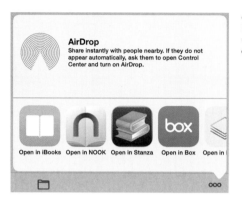

6.25 Scroll the horizontal list of apps until you find one that can open the file.

The other app opens, displaying the document (6.26).

6.26 This EPUB file opened just fine in iBooks.

Renaming files

You must select a file before you can rename it. Follow these steps:

1. In the OneDrive app, navigate so you can see the file you want to rename.

2. Tap the Actions button in the toolbar.

    A sheet appears with the possible actions you can take.

3. Tap Select Items.

    The screen changes to the Select Items screen (6.27).

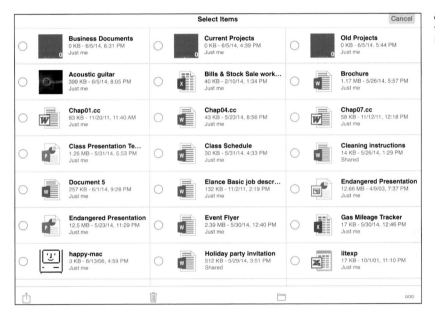

6.27 Begin renaming files in the Select Items screen.

4. Tap the selection circle next to the file you want to rename.

    You can rename only one file at a time.

5. Tap the Actions button, which is now in the toolbar at the bottom of the screen.

    A sheet appears with context-appropriate actions.

6. Tap Rename This File.

    The Rename sheet appears.

7. Change the file name in the Name field; then tap Done (6.28).

Rename **Done**

NAME

Endangered Presentation (old)

Shared

6.28 Type the new name in the Rename sheet.

The name of the file changes, and the OneDrive app keeps you in selection mode, in case you want to make other changes.

8. If you have no other changes, tap Cancel to exit selection mode.

Deleting and moving files

You use the OneDrive app almost exactly the same way to delete or move files as you do with folders. First, you select the file or files; then you delete or move them. I could repeat all those instructions again, but I refer you to "Deleting and moving folders" earlier in this chapter. Just imagine I wrote *file* where the steps say *folder*.

Sharing Files and Folders

You can share files and folders from the OneDrive app, in somewhat the same fashion that you share items from within the Office for iPad apps, as discussed in Chapter 4. You can share a link to a file or folder on your One-Drive via email, or you can copy a link to the Clipboard. You can also change the permissions on a file or folder to allow them to be shared by coworkers. The procedures for sharing folders and files are slightly different.

Sharing folders

Follow these steps to share a folder from the OneDrive app:

1. Navigate in the OneDrive app so that you are inside the folder you want to share.

2. Tap the Actions button in the toolbar.

   A sheet appears with context-appropriate actions (**6.29**).

6.29 Begin sharing a folder by tapping the context-sensitive Actions button.

3. Tap Sharing and Permissions.

   The sheet changes to show the next level of choices (**6.30**).

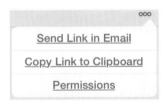

6.30 The sheet shows you the possible sharing choices.

4. Do one of the following:

   Tap Send Link in Email. The sheet changes to let you know the link can be View Only or View and Edit (**6.31**). Tap your choice. The OneDrive app creates the link and an email message sheet appears, containing the link. Address the email; then tap Send.

6.31 You can choose to restrict the sharing level of items you share.

or

Tap Copy Link to Clipboard. The sheet changes to let you know the link can be View Only or View and Edit. Tap your choice, and the One-Drive app creates the link and copies it to the Clipboard, ready for you to switch to another app and paste the link in.

or

Tap Permissions. The Permissions sheet appears, showing you the name of the folder and its current permissions (6.32). To share the folder with one or more coworkers, tap the Add People button (it looks like a plus sign). The Add People sheet appears (6.33). Tap the Plus button in the Share With field to bring up a list of your contacts; then tap their email addresses to add them to the Add People sheet. Under Options, you can choose to allow editing and state whether the recipient must have a Microsoft account to access the shared folder. Tap Add. One-Drive e-mails the selected coworkers invitations to share the folder.

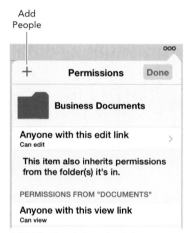

6.32 The Permissions sheet shows you the current permissions for the folder.

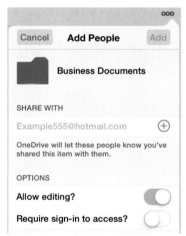

6.33 Add your coworkers in the Share With field.

Sharing files

Sharing files from the OneDrive app is just like sharing folders, except that you must select the file first, and you can only share one file at a time. In this section, I walk you through part of the process and then refer you to the sharing process in the preceding section. Follow these steps:

1. In the OneDrive app, navigate so you can see the file you want to rename.

2. Tap the Actions button in the toolbar.

   A sheet appears with the possible actions you can take.

3. Tap Select Items.

   The screen changes to the Select Items screen.

4. Tap the selection circle next to the file you want to share.

   You can share only one file at a time.

5. Tap the Share button, which is now in the toolbar at the bottom of the screen.

   A sheet appears with the sharing actions (6.34).

Selected file

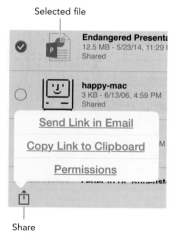

6.34 The Share button allows you to choose how you want to share the selected file.

Share

6. To take one of the sharing actions, see Step 4 of "Sharing folders" earlier in this chapter.

Refreshing Folders and Files

The contents of your OneDrive cloud storage change whenever you make changes on any of the devices you have connected to it. Although the OneDrive app automatically checks the server and refreshes its view of what's on your OneDrive frequently, there may be times when you're using the service on multiple devices at the same time and want to refresh your mobile device manually to make certain that you are up to date.

To manually refresh the view, tap and pull downward on any of the places where you can view folders or files on your OneDrive. For example, if you want to refresh the folders on your OneDrive, tap and drag the folder column down (6.35). When you pull the screen down, you can see the last time the view was updated. You see the standard "waiting" icon for a second at the top of the column; then the iPad checks with the OneDrive server, the view refreshes, and the column returns to normal.

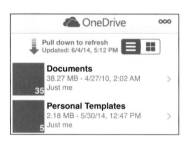

6.35 Tap and drag downward to manually refresh the view of your OneDrive.

Using the Other Tabs

Up to now, you've used the Files tab for everything you've done in this chapter. Here's a quick rundown of the other three tabs:

- **Camera Backup** is a view of all of the pictures from all of your connected iOS devices that have been backed up to OneDrive (6.36). Tap any of the pictures to open them in the OneDrive app's file viewer. You can select one or more images in this view and delete them or move them to a different folder.

6.36 The photos on your OneDrive appear in the Camera Backup tab.

- **Recent** is a chronological list of all the files you have worked on using the OneDrive app. One exception to this are files that you have worked with on the Camera Backup tab; those files don't appear in the Recent files tab.

- **Shared** shows you files or folders that other people have shared with you.

Using Settings

The gearlike Settings button in the bottom toolbar gives you some general information about your OneDrive account and the ability to turn some options on or off (6.37). You can also use Settings to sign out of OneDrive.

6.37 Use Settings to find out how much OneDrive space you have available and change other miscellaneous settings.

In the Settings sheet, you find the following:

- **Account** shows you the Microsoft account you are signed in to; it's the email address that serves as the username for your Microsoft account.

- **Storage** shows you how much of your OneDrive storage is in use.

Under Options, you can turn Camera Backup on or off, and have your Photo Downloads done at their original size or resized for quicker downloading.

The About section contains the version of the OneDrive app and some legal boilerplate.

If you scroll to the bottom of the Settings sheet, you find a Sign Out choice; tapping that option signs the OneDrive app out of your OneDrive account.

CHAPTER 7

Editing Documents with Office Online

Office Online is the name Microsoft uses for the limited versions of the Office apps that you can use online, with nothing more than a browser. Office Online is free for everyone. Even without an Office 365 subscription, you can use the Office Online apps to create, view, save, and print Office documents and then save them in a free (though limited) amount of OneDrive storage. These features make Office Online very similar to other productivity suites available through browsers, such as Google Drive (https://drive.google.com) and Zoho Office (www.zoho.com). When you add a subscription to Office 365 to the mix, you get additional OneDrive storage and access to the desktop and tablet versions of Office as well.

Office Online also has access to all your OneDrive storage, so if you have a subscription to Office 365, the changes you make online are immediately synchronized to all your other devices.

Office Online even works on devices such as Chromebooks, or in Safari or Chrome running on iPads. All you need to use any of the Office Online apps are a browser and an Internet connection. (You can't use Office Online if you aren't connected to the Internet.)

Finally, Office Online documents can be edited simultaneously by different people, and the Office apps keeps track of everyone's edits.

In this chapter, you see how you can use the Office Online apps to create documents, share your work with people who otherwise have no access to Office at all, and use Office Online apps to make quick changes in your own documents when you're away from your iPad or desktop machines running Office.

Using Office Online

To use Office Online, you need to sign in with (and if necessary, create) a Microsoft account, but it doesn't need to be the same Microsoft account that you use to access the rest of your Office 365 subscription. If you have a basic free Microsoft account, you get 15 GB of OneDrive storage as part of the free account.

The Office Online apps consist of stripped-down versions of the following programs:

- Word
- Excel
- PowerPoint
- OneNote

- Outlook
- Calendar
- People
- OneDrive

When I say *stripped-down,* I'm not talking about barely usable versions; you can do a lot with these browser-based apps. The apps have the familiar Ribbon and the rest of the user interface of the desktop-based versions. You won't be able to run macros or mail merges in Word, but those features aren't exactly part of the program's core features anyway.

To get started with Office Online, follow these steps:

1. Go to https://office.com in any modern browser—such as Mozilla Firefox, Internet Explorer, Google's Chrome, or Apple's Safari—running under any recent operating system (7.1).

7.1 Office Online works in any modern browser, and it's free to use.

2. Click the Sign In link at the top of the page.

3. On the next page, enter the email address of your Microsoft account, and click the Next button.

4. Type your password on the next screen, and click the Sign In button (7.2). You return to the main Office Online screen (refer to 7.1).

▶ **NOTE** You know when you've signed in to Office Online, because your username appears at the top of the page.

7.2 You need a Microsoft account to use the online goodies.

5. Click the icon of the app you want to use.

Creating a New Office Online Document

This section shows you how to create a new Office Online document. I use Word for the example, but the process for Excel or PowerPoint is similar.

To create a new document, follow these steps:

1. Click the icon for the app you want to use.

   For this exercise, click Word Online.

   Word, Excel, and PowerPoint all give you the same choices in the Let's Get Started screen (7.3). You can create a new blank document, create a document from Microsoft's built-in templates, or you can browse and open one of your documents on OneDrive.

2. For this exercise, click the Browse Templates button.

   The Templates for Word screen shows you a fairly large number of templates that you can use as jumping-off points for your own documents (7.4). They're not just useful, but also nicely designed, using Word's formatting features expertly. You can narrow the templates shown by clicking one of the categories on the left side of the page.

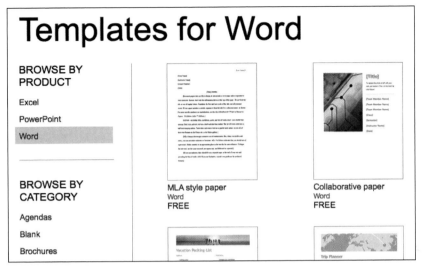

7.4 Microsoft provides a fairly large number of document templates to get you started.

3. For this exercise, click the Meeting Minutes template (not shown in 7.4).

   On the details page for the template you selected (7.5), the template's price is listed as Free. Microsoft charges for some templates, mostly those from third parties.

7.5 Each document template has a details page like this one.

4. Click Open in Word Online.

   An overlay dialog box lets you know that the template will be saved to your OneDrive.

5. Click the Continue button.

The template opens in Word Online in your browser (7.6). Because it's a template, the document contains many placeholders, which are shown as text inside square brackets .

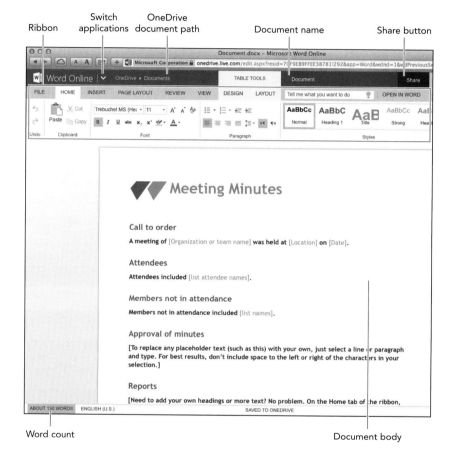

7.6 A Word Online document looks quite similar to Word running on a Windows PC or a Mac.

6. Replace the placeholder text by selecting it, including the brackets, and typing over it (7.7).

7.7 Replacing a placeholder.

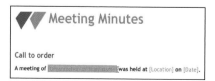 

7. To give your document a new title, click the title at the top of the page (*Document*, in this case) to select it; then type the new document title over it (7.8).

7.8 Select the document name (left) and then type a new one over it (right).

8. Click anywhere else on the page to save the title.

All the Office Online apps save your documents constantly and automatically; this particular document has now been saved to your OneDrive storage on all your devices. If you look in your OneDrive/Documents folder, you see that the document's name has changed on all your devices (7.9).

7.9 As soon as you rename a document inside Office Online, the change is pushed to all your OneDrive devices.

Touring a Word Online Document

Notice several important things about the Word Online Web application and the Word documents it creates:

- The app looks very much like Microsoft Word, with the familiar Ribbon and its formatting controls.

- The top bar displays the document's title and the path to the document.

- The bottom-left corner gives you an approximate word count—a useful feature for many writers.

Managing Office Online Documents

Office Online allows you to open, edit, rename, print, share, and access previous versions of documents. In this section, I show you how those features work.

Opening documents

To open a document in Office Online, follow these steps:

1. With any document open, click the File tab at the far-left edge of the Ribbon, which by default opens to the Open category (7.10).

    ▶ **TIP** If you click the wrong tab by mistake, click the Back button at the top of the tab to return to your document.

    You're shown the most recent documents.

Back
button

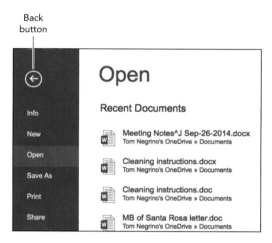

7.10 Clicking the File tab in Word Online takes you to the Open category by default.

2. Click a document's name to open it.

    If the document you want isn't shown, click the More on OneDrive link at the bottom of the document list to open the online OneDrive app in a new tab (7.11). Then you can navigate to and click the document you want; it opens in the Office Online application appropriate for that sort of document.

7.11 The OneDrive online app allows you to manage your documents.

3. Back on the File tab, click New to create a new blank document or a another new document from a template.

Renaming and printing documents

The File tab's Save As category doesn't work the way you might expect. Instead of allowing you to save the current document under a different name, it instead gives you controls that allow you to download a copy of the document from the cloud to your computer as an Office document or to download the current document to your computer as a PDF file.

Similarly, the Print category doesn't print the current document directly from your browser, because chances are that your browser won't preserve the document's formatting correctly. Instead, choose Print to create a PDF; then use Adobe's free Reader browser plug-in to display the PDF in a new browser tab and print it from there (7.12).

▶ **TIP** This printing capability may differ slightly, depending on the browser you're using to access Office Online. Google's Chrome browser, for example, displays its own PDF files rather than using Adobe's Reader plug-in, so the printing process takes place without the need to open a new browser tab.

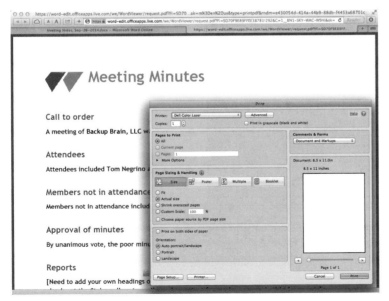

7.12 Printing from some browsers requires the free Adobe Reader browser plug-in.

Sharing documents

The File tab has a Share button, which I cover in "Sharing Your Office Online Documents" later in this chapter.

Editing documents

If you have a subscription to Office 365 and a desktop version of Word, the Info category of the File tab in Office Online allows you to switch the document to the full-featured version of Word for editing. Click the Info button at the top of the File tab to open the Info tab (7.13); then click Open in Word to open the document for editing in your desktop version of Word.

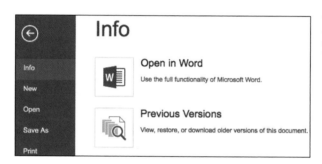

7.13 Open documents on your desktop computer from the Info tab.

Accessing earlier versions of documents

The Info tab (refer to 7.13 earlier in this chapter) also allows you to access previous versions of the document you're working on, which can be very useful, especially when you're editing a document collaboratively. Click the Info button at the top of the File tab to open the Info tab; then click Previous Versions.

Managing Documents with OneDrive Online

Choosing OneDrive from the application switcher (see "Managing Applications" later in this chapter) brings up the online OneDrive app **(7.14)**, which superficially resembles the iOS OneDrive app discussed in Chapter 6. But some differences between the tablet and Web versions of OneDrive are worth pointing out:

7.14 The OneDrive Online app allows you to manage the contents of your OneDrive storage.

- Like the iOS version, the Office Online OneDrive app shows you the folders you have in your OneDrive storage as tiles. One difference, however, is that the online version has a left-side sidebar that lets you filter for all files, recent files, or shared items. Double-clicking a folder shows you its contents, as you would expect.

- When no file is selected, the top bar of the OneDrive app offers Create, Upload, Share, and Folder Actions menus.

- Finally, when you move the mouse over a file, a check box appears over it, allowing you to select it. Then a new set of menus appears, offering options for managing the file.

Sharing Your Office Online Documents

Sharing is a big part of working with documents in OneDrive and on Office Online. You have two basic ways to share your documents:

- Invite one or more people to share a document with you by sending an email invitation that includes a link to the document.

- Post a link to the document in an email, in social media, or on a Web page.

Both methods let you choose whether the recipients of your invitation can merely view the shared document or also edit it.

▶ **NOTE** Sharing documents in Office Online is similar to the procedures I discuss in Chapter 6, but the differences call for covering the process here as well.

Sharing via email

Follow these steps to share your documents via email:

1. With your Office Online document open onscreen, click the Share button on the top bar of the document.

   or

   Click the File tab, click the Share button, and then click the Share with People button.

   The Share overlay appears, set to Invite People (7.15).

7.15 The Share overlay lets you get started sharing your documents.

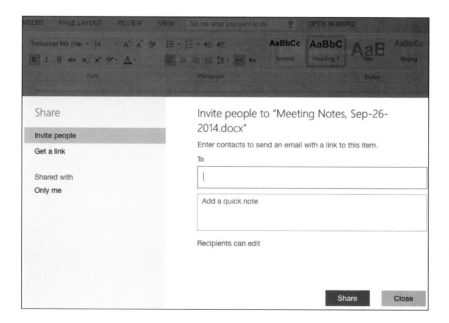

2. Type the name of one or more people in the To field.

   If these people are already in your online People address book, their names appear below the field as you type, and you can select those names to add them easily (7.16). Otherwise, type the full email addresses.

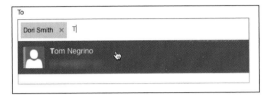

7.16 If certain people are already in your address book, Office Online previews their names as you type.

3. (Optional) Type a note explaining the invitation.

4. If you want the recipients to be able to edit the document, click the Recipients Can Edit link; choose an option from the first pop-up menu (Recipients Can Edit or Recipients Can Only View); and then choose an option from the second pop-up menu (Recipients Don't Need a Microsoft Account or Recipients Need to Sign in With a Microsoft Account).

5. Click Share to send your invitation.

   When you've sent the invitation, the Share overlay displays the recipients and their editing privileges (7.17). If you like, you can choose to change the editing privileges or even stop sharing the file altogether.

6. Click the Close button to dismiss the Share overlay.

7.17 You can change an invitee's document-editing privileges.

Sharing with a link on social media

If you want to post a link to your document on social media, follow these steps:

1. With your Office Online document open onscreen, click the Share button on the top bar of the document.

   The Share overlay appears (refer to 7.15 earlier in this chapter).

2. In the Share section, click Get a Link.

   The Share overlay changes to reflect your choice.

3. From the Choose an Option pop-up menu (7.18), choose the editing privileges you want to grant anyone who views the document: View Only, Edit, or Public.

4. Click Create Link.

The link appears, along with sharing buttons for Facebook, Twitter, LinkedIn, and Weibo (7.19).

▶ **TIP** The link is rather long, and you can create a less-unwieldy version by clicking Shorten Link.

7.19 The link appears on the Share overlay.

5. Copy the link and paste it into your blog editor.

Sharing by embedding a document in a Web page

If email and social media sharing aren't for you (see the preceding two sections), you can create a different sort of link that embeds your document in a Web page. Follow these steps to create this link:

1. With your Office Online document open onscreen, click the File tab on the Ribbon; then click the Share button to open the Share overlay.

2. Select Embed (7.20).

The Embed overlay appears (7.21).

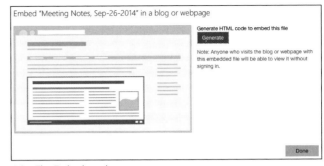

7.20 Click Embed on the File tab.

7.21 The Embed overlay.

3. Click the Generate button to create the HTML code you need for your embeddable document.

   Another Embed overlay appears, displaying a preview of your document and copyable HTML code (7.22).

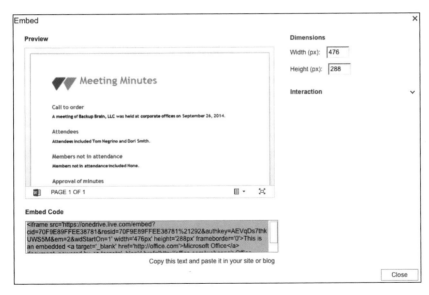

7.22 All the code you need to embed your document.

4. Copy the entire contents of the Embed Code box, and paste that code into your blog or Website editor.

5. Click the Close button to dismiss the Embed overlay.

Managing Applications and Services

You have access to all the Office Online apps whenever you're signed in to any of them. The easiest way to switch between apps is to click the Switch Applications arrow next to the name of the current app (refer to 7.6 earlier in this chapter). Doing so causes the application switcher to appear (7.23). Clicking the icons on this switcher makes it easy to jump to any other applications or services.

7.23 Navigate Office Online apps and services with the application switcher.

The application switcher also gives you quick access to other services that enhance your Office 365 experience. You can use Outlook.com to handle your email, schedule appointments and reminders with the Calendar service, and manage an online address book with the People application. You can also manage your documents with the OneDrive app (see the sidebar "Managing Documents with OneDrive Online" earlier in this chapter).

CHAPTER 8

Working with Text

Microsoft Word is the app that probably gets the most use in the Office suite, and it offers a wide array of features and capabilities that allow you to create just about any kind of document you can imagine. The version for iPad doesn't have all the features of Word for Mac or Windows, but you'll still find more than enough to get your work done. It's a mobile word processor that strikes a terrific balance between powerful features and ease-of-use.

In this chapter, you'll learn how to work with text in Word for iPad, how to find and replace text, and how to use headers and footers.

Adding Text

Start up Word, and the app assumes that you want to resume what you were doing when you last left. So, if you were previously editing a document, you'll go back to it.

Word's interface includes two main areas (8.1):

- The **Ribbon** contains the tabs for the different areas of the program in the toolbar to help you add and modify content. Above the Ribbon, you'll see the document title (if the document has been saved; otherwise, you'll see Document *x*).

- The **document area** is the main Word document window. It's where you'll edit your text and place graphics and tables.

As is the case with all of the Office for iPad apps, you should consider, whenever possible, starting with a template, which does much of the formatting for you and will save you a lot of time. Of course, you can always start with a blank sheet (conveniently called the New Blank Document template in the New tab of the file manager). See Chapter 5 for more about working with templates.

A Word about Feature Discussions

There are many operations that are similar across the Office for iPad apps, and I have limited space in this slim book, so rather than repeating the functions for each app, I've spread out the instructions across the different apps. For example, you add tables to your documents in much the same fashion in Word and PowerPoint, so when I discuss tables, you'll see how to add them in PowerPoint, in Chapter 15. Because PowerPoint presentations also make frequent use of pictures and shapes on slides, even though you can add pictures and shapes to Word documents, I also discuss them in Chapter 15. Similarly, there are reviewing and commenting features in Word, in Excel, and PowerPoint, but I am only discussing them in the context of Word, in Chapter 9. With all these common features, there may be some differences in detail between the different apps, but you'll find those differences are easy to figure out.

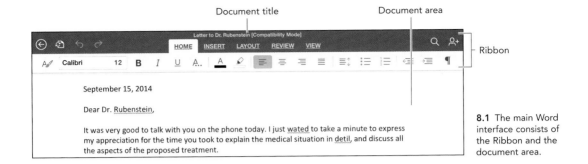

Document title · Document area

Ribbon

8.1 The main Word interface consists of the Ribbon and the document area.

Entering and editing text

You enter and edit text in Word much as you do in any other iOS app. Simply tap in the document area and begin typing, either using the onscreen keyboard or with an external Bluetooth keyboard (though for longer documents, you'll find the external hardware much easier to use).

To select text, hold a word in the document area for a second then release it, which brings up the Selection popover (8.2). Besides the usual Select, Select All, and Paste commands, the Insert command in Word allows you to add a tab or a line break at the selection point.

To select a particular word, double-tap the word, which selects it and brings up the Edit popover (8.3). As usual, you can extend the selection by dragging the word selection handles, and you can use the commands in the Edit popover to move text to or from the Clipboard. To quickly select an entire paragraph, triple-tap within the paragraph. The best way to clear a text selection is to tap in the left or right margins, because that way you don't accidentally move the insertion point.

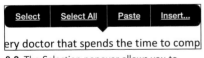

8.2 The Selection popover allows you to select a single word or all the words in the document.

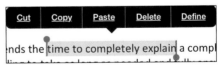

8.3 The Edit popover allows you to move text to and from the Clipboard,.

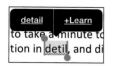

8.4 After you select a misspelled word, the Suggestion popover lets you fix a mistake or add the word to Word's user dictionary.

Misspelled words appear with the familiar wavy red underline. To fix them, double-tap the word to make the Suggestion popover appear **(8.4)**. Word usually has one or more suggestions; tap the one you want to replace the misspelled word with the suggestion. If instead the word should be added to Word's user dictionary, tap the +Learn choice in the popover.

Styling text

When you need to style text, you have the tools in the Home tab of the Ribbon available to you **(8.5)**. To style text, follow these steps:

1. Select the text you want to style.

2. Use the controls in the Home tab of the Ribbon to make your desired changes.

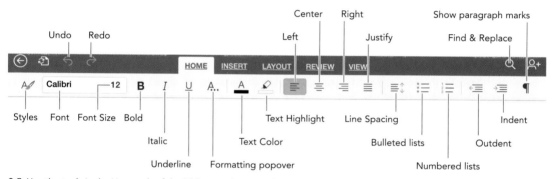

8.5 Use the tools in the Home tab of the Ribbon to do most of your text formatting.

> ▶ **TIP** Sometimes it can be a little difficult to work accurately with text, especially if you're just trying to style one letter at a time. Don't forget that you can pinch or spread your fingers on the screen to zoom the screen for easier viewing. If that's not enough, you can always select part or even all of the text in your document, temporarily increase the font size to ludicrous-but-visible levels, make your changes, then revert the font size to normal. You can also get a better view of where the end of the paragraph is by tapping the Show Paragraph Marks control on the Home tab of the ribbon, which displays the non-printing paragraph marks **(8.6)**.

> ¶
>
> Dear Dr. Rubenstein, ¶
>
> ¶
>
> It was very good to talk with you on the p
> my appreciation for the time you took to
> the aspects of the proposed treatment. ¶
>
> ¶

8.6 Sometimes it makes it easier to edit your text to show the invisible paragraph marks.

Dealing with Word Styles

In Microsoft Word for Mac or Windows, a *style* is a collection of formatting commands that are grouped together and given a name, which you can apply with a single click. Word on the desktop has two types of styles. *Character styles* can be a combination of any of the character formats that you can apply from the Ribbon or Font dialog. Character styles are usually applied to individual words or blocks of words within paragraphs. Paragraph styles can be a combination of character formatting and paragraph formatting, including text alignment, indents, tab stops, and other kinds of formatting. *Paragraph formats* apply to an entire paragraph at a time. They are also the most often used type of styles.

Styles are one of the components of document templates, and Word for iPad has both good and bad news when it comes to styles. The bad news is that you cannot add or customize styles with the iPad app. The good news is that you can usually view styles on the iPad that are contained in documents that you import from Word on Windows or Mac, and the representation of those files is usually pretty good. Sometimes you can even apply existing styles using Word for iPad, either paragraph or character styles, from the Styles popover on the Home tab of the Ribbon (8.7).

But I have found in my testing that if your Word document uses complex stylesheets with many named styles, even though the styles display well in Word for iPad, the style names often will not appear in the Styles popover, leaving you no way to actually apply the styles to documents on the iPad. One workaround that sometimes works is to copy the style and then use the Paste Format command in the Edit popover to apply it. But I have not found this to work consistently, indicating that there are bugs Microsoft still needs to fix.

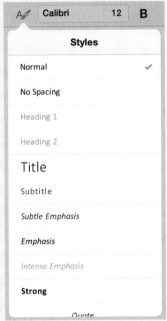

8.7 The Styles popover shows the styles available to you that can be applied in the current document.

Working with Lists

It's often the case that facts or procedures can be described in a few steps, or as a list. With some facts, the order in which they are presented isn't important; but with procedures, order is sometimes all-important. For example, you wouldn't want to be on the wrong end of this procedure: Ready; Fire; Aim! Word gives you tools for both ordered (numbered) and unordered (bulleted) lists.

You can apply either kind of list formatting to already existing text, or you can apply it as you compose text. Word even allows you to mix numbered and bulleted lists.

To apply a list to existing text, follow these steps:

1. Select existing text in your document.

2. On the Home tab of the Ribbon, tap either Bulleted lists or Numbered lists.

   The corresponding popover appears (8.8).

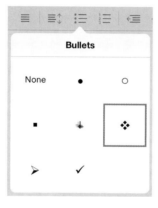

8.8 For this list, I'm using the Bullets popover.

3. In the popover, choose the style you want for the list.

   The text changes to reflect your choice (8.9).

Planets of the Solar System	Planets of the Solar System
Mercury	❖ Mercury
Venus	❖ Venus
Earth	❖ Earth
Mars	❖ Mars
Jupiter	❖ Jupiter
Saturn	❖ Saturn
Uranus	❖ Uranus
Neptune	❖ Neptune

8.9 This list as it appears before bulleting (left) and after (right).

If instead you want to enter a list and have Word automatically insert numbers or bullets for you, follow these steps:

1. On the Home tab of the Ribbon, tap either Bulleted lists or Numbered lists.

   The corresponding popover appears (8.10).

8.10 I'm going to be creating a numbered list by choosing a numbering style in the Numbering popover.

2. Tap the number or bullet style you want to use.

3. Begin typing your list. At the end of each line, press Return, and Word will begin the next line with the number or bullet style you chose (8.11).

1960's Space Programs

1. Mercury
2. Gemini
3. Apollo

8.11 The numbers and the period following them were automatically generated by Word.

Word automatically does multi-level lists; you can create them by pressing the Tab key right after you press Return. For example, in 8.11, had I pressed the Tab key right after I entered "Mercury" and pressed Return, Word would have automatically created a sublist that began with "a." To return to the main list after you have been entering items in a sublist, press Shift-Tab.

4. Press the Return key twice to exit the list.

▶   **TIP** To mix list types, create the list using the list type you want to use the most. Then go back and select the lines you want to format in the other list type, then choose that list type from the Ribbon.

Finding and Replacing Text

When your company changes the name of your main product, you'll be happy that Word allows you to find and replace text. One drawback of the iPad version is that though you can replace text, you can't search for and replace formatting.

To get started finding and replacing text, follow these steps:

1. Tap the Find & Replace icon on the Ribbon.

    The Ribbon disappears and is replaced with the search bar (8.12). Initially, the search bar appears set only to Find. If you would rather find and replace, tap the Options control and switch to Find and Replace mode from the Options popover (8.13). In this example, I'll be finding and replacing.

Options   Find field   Replace field   Replace All   Previous
                               Replace   Next

🔍 **Apple**   7   **Orange**   Replace   All   <   >

8.12 Begin finding and replacing text in the search bar.

8.13 Besides switching modes between Find and Find and Replace, you can modify the way Word finds the text.

2. Tap into the Find field, and enter your search text.

3. Tap into the Replace field, and enter your replacement text.

   Word automatically finds and highlights the first instance of the search text, and also counts and inserts the number of instances of the search text into the Find field.

4. Depending on what you want to do, use the Replace, All, Previous, or Next buttons to work through finding and replacing the text in your document.

5. Exit search mode by tapping in the document area.

Getting Word Counts

In many forms of writing, you'll be asked to write either a minimum or maximum number of pages, words, or characters. For example, you could be writing an article for a magazine or online publication and be asked to produce (and be paid for) a maximum number of words. Having dealt with, over the years, many an editor who gets cranky when I write too many words, I'm happy that Word for iPad has a Word Count ability.

To discover the length of your document, follow these steps:

1. Open the document you want to check.

2. Tap the View tab on the Ribbon.

3. Tap Word Count.

The Word Count popover appears, showing the number of pages, words, and characters in your document (the latter with and without the spaces) (8.14).

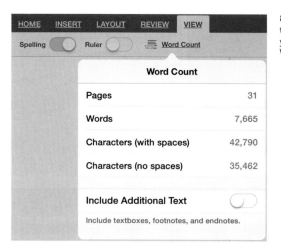

8.14 The View tab of the Ribbon is where you'll find Word's Word Count feature.

CHAPTER 9

Formatting and Collaboration

Professional documents require accurate content and a professional look. When it comes to formatting a document, typically less is more; you don't want to overwhelm the reader with all kinds of fancy formatting techniques. When you create a document in Word, you should pay particular attention to the impression the layout of your document creates. Is it interesting and consistent or is it loud and confused? You'll often find that colleagues can be extremely helpful with feedback when it comes to formatting, not to mention the content of your document.

In this chapter, we'll look at formatting paragraphs using the Ruler to set up indents and tabs. You'll see how to create and edit headers and footers. And we'll delve into document collaboration with your coworkers, including adding comments and working with change tracking.

Working with the Ruler

When you create a document, most of the time you'll present your text in the standard, left-aligned format that reaches from margin to margin. But some paragraphs require you to change the line wrap for quotations, add some tab stops, change the indent of the first line of a paragraph, and more. Word's Ruler shows your document's margins, the right and left indents for the current paragraph, the position of the first line indent, and any tab stops present in the paragraph you're editing (9.1).

By default, the Ruler is turned off, to make the maximum use of the iPad's limited screen real estate. To display the Ruler, tap the View tab in the Ribbon, then slide the Ruler switch to the on position.

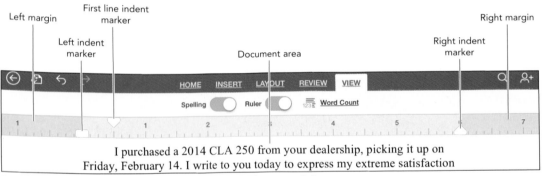

9.1 The Ruler shows you the invisible formatting that controls paragraph formats.

Using the Ruler to set indents

The left and right indents of a paragraph indicate where the first character of the paragraph will be placed and the point beyond which a word wraps to the next line of the document. You can position the indents using the Ruler by dragging the indent marker to the desired location.

Tap inside a single paragraph or select text in multiple paragraphs for which you want to set the indent, and then do any of the following:

- Drag the Left indent marker to the place where you want the left edge of the paragraph to begin.

- Drag the Right indent marker to the location where you want the right edge of the paragraph. If any characters in a word would be written to the right of this boundary, the whole word will be wrapped to the next line.

- Drag the First line indent marker to the location where you want the first line of the paragraph to begin. All subsequent lines in the paragraph will begin at the left indent marker.

- You can create a *hanging indent* by dragging the First line indent marker to the left of the Left indent marker. When you create a hanging indent, the second and subsequent lines of the paragraph begin to the right of where the first line began. Hanging indents are most often used in bulleted and numbered lists to place the item marker to the left of the item's text (9.2).

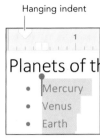

9.2 In the Ruler, moving the first line indent marker to the left of the left margin marker creates a hanging indent.

Using the Ruler to set tabs

Another way you can use the Ruler to format paragraphs in your document is to set *tab stops*. A tab stop (a somewhat old-fashioned term reminiscent of the days of typewriters) is a location you set to use as a guide to placing text in a line of your document. For example, you can make the date of the document appear near the right margin, or you can use multiple tabs to create columns of data in your document, as in a price list. **Table 9.1** describes the different tab stops that are available and how they are used, and (9.3) shows the marker of each tab type as it appears in the Ruler.

9.3 The different tab markers in the Ruler show Left, Center, Right, Decimal, and Bar tabs.

Table 9.1 Available Tab Types

Tab Type	Description
Left Tab	Text starts at the tab and continues to the right until it reaches the end of the line. Any text in the paragraph that spills over to the next line begins at the left indent marker.
Center Tab	Text is centered on the tab stop.
Right Tab	Text begins at the tab stop and moves to the left as you type.
Decimal Tab	Columns of numbers are aligned on the decimal point.
Bar Tab	A vertical line (bar) is placed on every line where the tab stop is in effect. This is used to draw vertical lines on a page.

To use the ruler for a portion of your document, follow these steps:

1. Select the portion of the document to which you want to assign tab stops.

2. In the Ruler, tap once where you want your tab to appear.

   By default, a marker for a Left tab appears on the Ruler. Double-tap the tab marker to cycle the tab stop through the different tab types until you get the kind of tab you want.

3. If you don't get the tab in exactly the right spot, drag it to the correct location on the Ruler.

   As you drag, a tool tip appears showing you the exact location of the tab stop.

4. Repeat as necessary to add additional tabs to the paragraph.

5. (Optional) To remove a tab, drag it from the Ruler to the body of your document.

9.4 It's easier to make sure you have added the correct tab characters by making them visible.

Item #	Description	Price
101	Wonder Widget	$149.95
102	Ginormous Gadget	$25.95
103	Classic Rubber Chicken	$9.95

Working with Headers and Footers

If you have text or other information you want to appear at the top or bottom of each printed page, you can add that information to the *headers* and *footers* of your document. Headers and footers exist by default in your document, but you must enter an editing mode to work with the content inside them.

To work with a header or footer in your document, follow these steps:

1. On the Layout tab of the Ribbon, tap Header & Footer.

    The Header & Footer popover appears (9.5).

    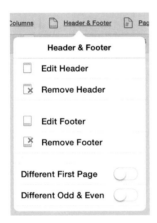

    9.5 Begin editing headers and footers with the Header & Footer popover.

2. Tap either Edit Header or Edit Footer.

    The header or footer area appears in the document window with a label and a line showing the area (9.6). By default, based on the New Blank Document template, headers and footers have a center tab and a right tab, as shown in the figure.

    9.6 When you are in editing mode, Word shows you the header or footer.

3. Enter the text you want in the header or footer. You can style the text as you wish, and you can also add or change tabs as needed.

4. Exit header or footer editing mode by tapping the Close control in the header or footer line.

▶ **TIP** You can also enter header or footer editing mode by double-tapping the very top or bottom of the page.

You get additional control over headers and footers in the Header & Footer popover. By turning on the Different First Page switch, you can suppress headers or footers for the first page of your document, or even have entirely differently formatted headers and footers on the first page. Similarly, by turning on the Different Odd & Even switch, you can change the headers and footers for odd or even numbered pages (of course, you will need to format the first instance of each odd or even page, after which Word will remember your preferences).

Inserting Page Numbers

You can add page numbers to your documents to enable readers to find and refer others to information easily, and to help keep document pages in order. To add page numbers to a document, follow these steps:

1. On the Layout tab of the Ribbon, tap Page Numbers.

   The Page Numbers popover appears (9.7).

9.7 You control page numbering and formatting with this popover.

2. If it isn't already switched on, slide the Numbering switch to the on position, which makes the additional controls below appear.

3. (Optional) If you want the page number to appear on the first page of your document, turn on the Show # on First Page switch.

4. (Optional) Choose the Position, Alignment, and Format of the page numbers.

   Position allows you to put the page numbers in either the header or the footer. Alignment allows you to choose whether the page numbers should be aligned to the left, center, right, or inside or outside the left or right document margins. Format allows you to choose between Arabic numbers, uppercase or lowercase letters, and the like.

   When you have finished with your settings, the page number appears in the document header or footer.

▶ **TIP** Page numbers are actually Word fields (a placeholder for data that Word updates automatically) and you can add text to the field, which allows you to add, for example, a prefix of "Page" to the page number. Tap on the page number in the header or footer until a selection box appears around it, then type the prefix or suffix text you want (9.8). That text will then appear as part of the page number.

9.8 You can add text to the field box that contains the automatic page numbering.

Document Markup and Review

Microsoft Word has powerful tools for collaborating, including tools to track changes, make comments, and track revisions made by different editors. Revisions are shown as text crossed out and added, and comments are shown by notes in the margin. Word gives you the tools to step through both comments and revisions, accepting or rejecting them as you see fit.

Word keeps its collaboration tools on the Review tab on the Ribbon (9.9). You can use the tools in this tab to turn change tracking on or off, work with comments, choose what kinds of changes appear in the document, and step through changes made by editors one by one.

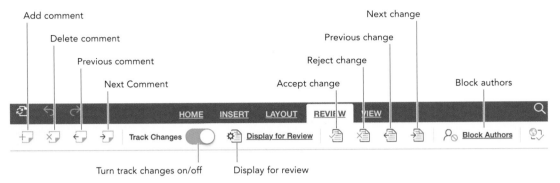

9.9 You'll find all of Word's collaboration tools on the Review tab of the Ribbon.

Working with comments

Using Word comments, coworkers can add as much text as they want to your documents, inserting comments that appear in a balloon that is linked to specific points in your text. Unlike revisions added using the Track Changes feature, comments don't markup the text with a strikethrough and colored changed text. Use comments when you want to add queries to the text, not when you actually want to suggest specific changes.

To add a comment, tap in a document or select the text where you want the comment to appear, then tap the Add Comment icon in the Ribbon. Word highlights the commented text, zooms the document out and creates a reviewing column at the right side of the document, and your comment appears in the reviewing column (9.10). Each commenter gets their own color, to make it easier to tell who's saying what when there are multiple commenters in a document.

9.10 Commented text gets highlighted and a line drawn to the comment in the reviewing column.

The rest of the commenting controls are straightforward. You can step through each comment using the Next Comment and Previous Comment icons, and you can remove comments using the Delete Comment icon, which has a popover that allows you to delete the current comment, delete all the comments currently being shown (you have the ability to show comments from certain editors), or delete all the comments in the document.

Tracking changes

When you turn on the Track Changes feature, any changes in the document are clearly marked. The main purpose of tracking changes is to enable the original author to see changes made to it and, when reviewing the document, decide whether to accept or reject them. Changes are shown in different colors, according to the people who made them. Deleted text is displayed in strikethrough style, and added text is underlined.

You enable change tracking in Word by sliding the Track Changes switch to the on position. Next, you need to decide which changes you will be reviewing. Tap the Display for Review icon in the Ribbon. In this popover (9.11), All Markup will show you all the comments and changes made to the document, using colored text for insertions and strikethroughs. No Markup shows you the document as if you had accepted all the proposed changes. Original with Markup shows the original text with tracked changes and comments. Original shows the original document as if all tracked changes had been rejected.

To give you additional control over the revisions you are reviewing, tap Show Markup at the bottom of the Display for Review popover. The popover changes to show you different categories of markup you can show or hide (9.12). Make your changes here as needed.

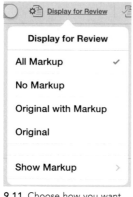

9.11 Choose how you want to look at your document containing tracked changes with this popover.

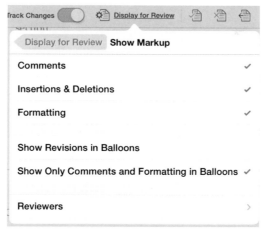

9.12 You can narrow the kind of tracked changes you are reviewing, and even ignore particular reviewers, with this popover.

To review tracked changes in your documents, follow these steps:

1. Tap to set the insertion point at the beginning of the document.

2. On the Review tab of the Ribbon, tap Next Change.

   Word highlights the first marked change in your document.

3. Tap either Accept Change or Reject Change.

   Depending on which you chose, the Accept or Reject popover appears (9.13). They are similar, so I will only show the Accept popover.

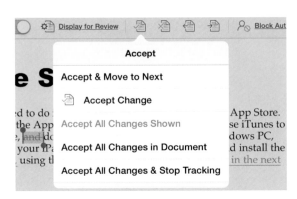

9.13 The highlighted deletion to the left of the popover is about to be accepted, and the process will eventually get to the underlined text to the popover's right.

4. Make your choice from the popover:

   - Accept & Move to Next accepts the change and moves to the next tracked change without you needing to tap the Next Change icon.

   - Accept Change accepts the current change, but does not change the position of the insertion point.

   - Accept All Changes Shown only becomes active if you have made changes in the Show Markup popover in 9.12.

   - Accept All Changes in Document allows you to accept all tracked changes with one tap.

   - Accept All Changes & Stop Tracking accepts all the tracked changes in the current document and turns Track Changes off.

CHAPTER 10

Changing Document Layout

In previous chapters we've talked about changing the formatting of specific elements of your document, but there will be times when you want to apply a specific format to your entire document in one fell swoop. For example, you might want to expand the margins of your document so that more text can appear on a single line, or change the orientation of the entire document so that the long edge of the paper, not the short edge, is on top.

In this chapter, you'll see how to change the margins of your documents; adjust the size of your virtual paper; insert page breaks and add sections; and reflow the text of your document into columns.

Working with Margins

Just as you can set indents for individual paragraphs in your text, you can set the minimum whitespace, called *margins*, that Word leaves at the edges of your document when you print it. Though margins are primarily involved with printing, Word also attempts to format your text on the screen to respect the margins so you have a better idea of your document's layout. Word for iPad uses the same margin presets as Word 2013 for Windows, as shown in **Table 10.1**.

Table 10.1 Margin Settings

Setting	Left	Right	Top	Bottom
Normal	1"	1"	1"	1"
Narrow	0.5"	0.5"	0.5"	0.5"
Moderate	0.75"	0.75"	1"	1"
Wide	2"	2"	1"	1"
Mirrored	1.25" (Inside)	1" (Outside)	1"	1"
Office 2003 Default	1.25"	1.25"	1"	1"

To use one of these preset margins, tap Margins on the Layout tab of the Ribbon. In the resulting Margins popover, choose the margin preset you want (10.1). The Mirrored preset needs a little explanation: it is designed so that the margins of the left page are a mirror image of those on the right page, so that a two-page spread looks balanced when it is printed. As a result, the inside margins are the same width and the outside margins are the same width.

Changing Your Virtual Paper

Depending on the type of document you are creating and your target audience, you might need to print its contents on paper other than the standard US Letter size (8.5" × 11"). Word lets you choose from a variety of paper sizes, including the most common European sizes, so if you have the right paper, you can print out accurately. You can also switch the orientation of your document so that your text prints across the long edge of the page ("Landscape") instead of the short edge ("Portrait").

To change the orientation of your page, tap Orientation on the Layout tab of the Ribbon. In the resulting Orientation popover, choose Portrait or Landscape **(10.2)**.

On the same Layout tab, to change the page size, tap Size, then choose the paper size you need from the Size popover **(10.3)**.

10.1 Word for iPad uses the same six margin presets as Word 2013 for Windows.

10.2 Flip your page direction with the Orientation popover.

10.3 You have your choice of seven common paper sizes in the Size popover.

Adding Page and Section Breaks

Sometimes you need to format your document so you don't have part of it stretch over two pages. For example, it's usually best if all of a table is on the same page, rather than have it start on one page and end on the next. Or you might be starting a new section of your document with a heading, and you want to make sure the heading and the first paragraph of the text beneath it are on the same page. In cases like this, you can manually insert a *page break*, which will tell Word to start a new page (and also start a new paragraph).

Word for iPad shows you a close representation of what the page will look like when printed, including the top and bottom margins (10.4). In this figure, only two lines from the last paragraph on the first page appear on the second page. I think things would look better if the entire last paragraph was pushed down onto the second page, so I'm going to insert a manual page break before the start of that paragraph. Follow these steps to add a page break:

1. Tap to position the insertion point at the location where you want to insert the page break.

2. On the Insert tab of the Ribbon, tap Breaks. From the resulting Breaks popover, tap Page (10.5).

    The page break is inserted, and the subsequent text moves down. Normally the page break marker is invisible, but you can make it visible (on screen; it won't print) by tapping the Show Paragraph Marks icon on the Home tab of the Ribbon (10.6).

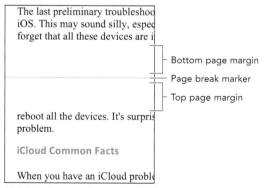

10.4 Word tries to show you a good representation of how text will fit on a page, including the top and bottom margins.

10.5 Use the Breaks popover to insert your page break.

10.6 By turning on viewing of paragraph marks, you can also see where Word inserts its invisible page break markers.

Adding page breaks is fine if you only need to change the appearance of a few words or a paragraph. But some formatting changes, such as margins, text alignment, and headers and footers are usually applied to your entire document. Word makes it possible for you to apply those changes to a portion of your document by defining document *sections*. In a document that has multiple sections, when you make a change that would normally affect the entire document, the change will affect only the selected section. This allows you to have parts of your document with entirely different margins, or even parts that are formatted to print in landscape mode, and have all of those different formatting choices contained in a single document.

To add a section to a document, you have to define what part of the document is a different section, and you do that by inserting a *section break*. Word allows you to create four kinds of section breaks:

- **Next Page** inserts a section break and has the next section begin on the next page.

- **Continuous** inserts a section break and has the next section begin on the line after the break.

- **Even Page** inserts a section break and has the next section break begin on the next even-numbered page. Formatting that you change in this kind of section affects only even-numbered pages.

- **Odd Page** inserts a section break and has the next section break begin on the next odd-numbered page. Formatting that you change in this kind of section affects only odd-numbered pages.

The Even Page and the Odd Page section breaks might cause you to have a blank page in your document, but they are ideal for when you want the next section to begin on a left-hand or right-hand page, respectively.

To insert a section break, position the insertion point at the desired location, then on the Insert tab of the Ribbon, tap Breaks. From the Breaks popover (see 10.5), tap the kind of section break you want.

Adding Columns

Letters, corporate reports, memos, and academic papers are almost always single-column documents, but other document types, notably newsletters, take advantage of columns to fit the maximum amount of text onto the page. Word for iPad allows you to format your text in five column types: One, Two, Three, Left, and Right. The first three are self-explanatory, but the Left choice gives you two columns with the left column taking up about a third of the horizontal space, and the right column taking up approximately $2/3$ of the space. The Right column type reverses the column proportions.

All of these column types produce "snaking" text, where the bottom of one column's text continues at the top of the next column. You get a little less flexibility with Word for iPad then you do with Word For Windows or Mac. You can't set a line in between columns on the iPad, nor can you specify the width of columns numerically. You are limited to a maximum of 3 columns, instead of the 12 on the desktop versions, but that's hardly a major restriction.

▶ **TIP** When creating columns, make sure that your columns are wide enough to allow at least five words per line. Any fewer words per line and the reader's eyes will move from line to line so frequently that it disrupts their reading.

To change your document to use columns, place the insertion point anywhere in the document, then tap Columns on the Layout tab of the Ribbon. In the resulting Columns popover, choose the column preset you want (10.7). The text is formatted appropriately (10.8).

10.7 Pick how many columns you want from the Columns popover.

10.8 Word for iPad creates the columns, but you don't have control over the width of the space between columns.

Sometimes when you're using columns, you can end up with unwanted layout problems, similar to page layout issues. For example, in 10.9, you can see that the header for a part of the document is marooned on the page before the section itself, which isn't good in terms of readability. You can push text into the next column by inserting a column break. It's better to use a column break in a situation like this instead of a page break, because if you reformat your document later, if you have a page break at that point you could end up with a blank page in the middle of your document.

First, in order for backups to work correctly, you have to have at least 100 MB of space free on your iOS device. Personally, I get nervous whenever I	**Fixing Problems with Contacts**
You could have any number of problems with contacts. For example, an app that you installed	Depending on how severe your problems are, you

10.9 The header in the right column of the top page is lonely, so we'll add a column break to reunite it with its section.

Follow these steps to add a column break:

1. Tap to position the insertion point at the location where you want to insert the column break.

2. On the Insert tab of the Ribbon, tap Breaks. From the resulting Breaks popover, tap Column (see 10.5).

   The text is reformatted as you command (10.10).

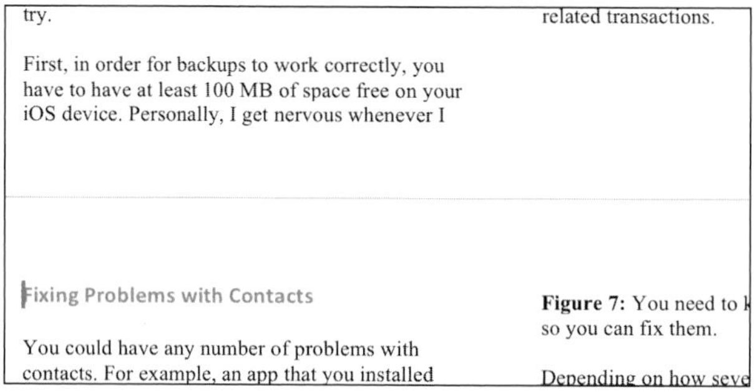

try.

First, in order for backups to work correctly, you have to have at least 100 MB of space free on your iOS device. Personally, I get nervous whenever I

related transactions.

10.10 After the column break, the header and its section are together, improving readability.

Fixing Problems with Contacts

You could have any number of problems with contacts. For example, an app that you installed

Figure 7: You need to k so you can fix them.

Depending on how sev

CHAPTER 11

Working with Worksheets

Microsoft Excel for iPad is a worksheet application, perfect for calculating, organizing, and analyzing your data. Every blank worksheet in Excel opens worlds of possibilities, with a tremendous amount of power under the hood. Because building worksheets can be time-consuming, you can and should use Excel templates to get a big jump on your calculating and data analyzing needs. See Chapter 5 for more about using templates.

In previous years, Microsoft focused Excel's abilities on raw calculation power and other traditional spreadsheet tasks. But they've embraced the reality that people love to use Excel to manage lists with a little calculation thrown in, so you'll find many templates of that type. They've also focused on how you can pull *meaning* out of your data through good visualization, and again, that's reflected in the templates.

In this chapter, I'll introduce you to Excel's interface; how to create workbooks and add worksheets to those workbooks; how you can enter and select data in a worksheet's cells; and how you can work with rows and columns.

Getting Started with Excel

When you open a new Excel document (perhaps from the New Blank Workbook template), you see the default *workbook* displayed with the Sheet1 worksheet visible. You can add additional worksheets to your workbook by tapping the New worksheet icon at the bottom of the screen. You can create calculations that draw data from different worksheets in a workbook, so often you'll have a workbook that contains a main or summary worksheet and several supporting worksheets that are used for data entry or supplementary calculations. In this figure (11.1), I'm using an example from one of the built-in templates to make it easier to view the different parts of the workbook. This worksheet has been renamed to "Ledger," and you can rename any worksheet by double-tapping the worksheet tab and typing your desired worksheet name.

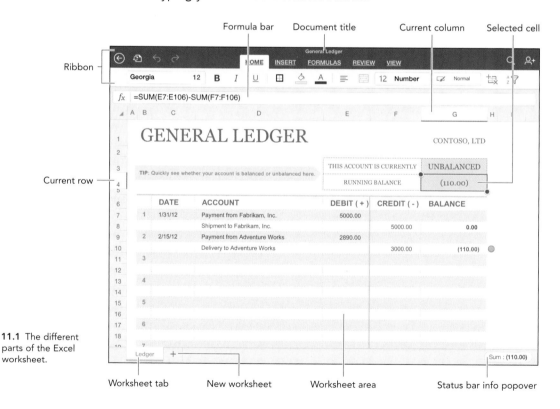

11.1 The different parts of the Excel worksheet.

A worksheet is easily recognizable by its column and row headers and its gridlines. The gridlines represent the physical boundaries of the *cells*, which contain numbers and formulas. Each cell is referenced by its cell name: these names are made up of a combination of their cell's column reference and its row reference, (i.e. the figure's G4). Excel for iPad can't create named cells or cell ranges (such as "Gross Profit"), but if they have been created on Excel for Windows or Mac, Excel for iPad can work with them.

Like the rest of the Office for iPad apps, Excel sports the Ribbon at the top of the screen, split into tabs. You'll be spending most of your time with the Home tab of the Ribbon, which is mainly devoted to formatting cells and their contents (11.2).

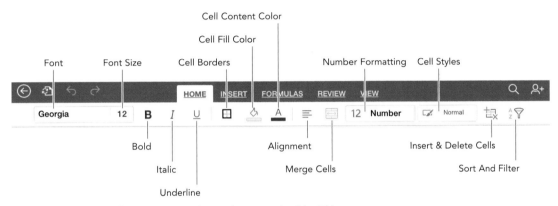

11.2 You'll spend most of your time in Excel using the Home tab of the Ribbon.

Under the Ribbon you'll find the *formula bar*, a special toolbar that you use to enter and edit formulas, data, and text in cells. When possible, Excel helps you build formulas by color coding cells and their corresponding cell references in the formula bar (11.3). As you can also see from the figure, you can enter formulas in either the formula bar or directly in the cell. You'll learn more about building formulas in Chapter 12.

	C	D	E
25	$ 97,493.50	$ 97,520.70	=D25-C25

fx =D25 - C25

11.3 The formula bar helps you visualize your formulas by color coding cell references whenever possible.

Down in the lower right corner of the screen is the status bar info icon, which gives you useful information about selected cells. To use it, select a range of cells by tapping the first cell and dragging to the last, then tap the status bar info icon. The resulting popover gives you six bits of information about the selected range of cells (11.4). In the figure, note the check mark next to Sum; you can tap next to any item in the popover and that information will then automatically display in the status bar without needing to invoke the popover.

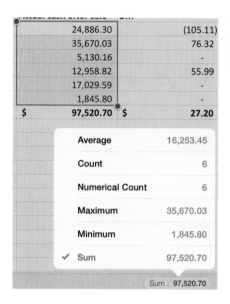

11.4 You can quickly get information about a cell range with the status bar info popover.

As mentioned before, you can add a new worksheet to your workbook by tapping the new worksheet icon at the bottom of the screen. To delete a worksheet you no longer need, tap the worksheet's tab once to switch to it, then tap it again to display the worksheet editing popover (11.5). You can also use this popover to duplicate or hide the current worksheet. To display a hidden worksheet, tap a visible worksheet's tab, then tap Unhide from the resulting popover, which then changes the popover to display the names of any hidden worksheets. Then tap the name of the worksheet you want to display.

11.5 You can delete worksheets you no longer need with the worksheet editing popover.

Excel for iPad Limitations

If you're a hardcore worksheet warrior, there's going to be some important limitations in Excel for iPad you will need to keep in mind, even though it is probably the most powerful mobile worksheet app available. In many cases, you can view features or data structures created with Excel for Windows or Mac, but you won't be able to change them. In effect, you can think of Excel for iPad as an excellent *player* of Excel features, but not a fully-capable *editor*. Some examples:

- Macros can't be run, because there's no VBA (Visual Basic for Applications) on the iPad.

- Conditional Formatting in cells can be viewed, but not added or updated.

- Sparklines in cells can be viewed, but not added or updated.

- Pivot Tables can be viewed, but not added, changed, sorted, or filtered.

- Data Validation works, but you can't add or update the restrictions for data in those cells.

- For data sorting and filtering, Slicers and Timelines are not supported.

- You can't use external datafiles to update your worksheets.

- You can't work on worksheets in two different workbooks at the same time, though you can of course work with multiple worksheets in the same workbook.

- Comments can be viewed and deleted, but not added or changed.

- You can't split windows, or have more than one at a time.

- The initial view of the document is always 150%, instead of how you last left the document.

Selecting and Entering Data

To activate a cell, you must select it, which you do by tapping the cell. The *active cell* is one where you can enter data or formulas in the Formula Bar, and you can only have one active cell at a time. You can tell a cell is selected or active because it has selection handles at its upper left and lower right corners (see 11.1). To extend the selection beyond a single cell, drag one of the selection handles until your selection encompasses the cell range you want (11.6). This also brings up the Edit popover, which allows you to cut, copy, or clear the cell range (we'll discuss fill later in this section).

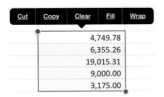

11.6 Use the Edit popover to move cell values and formatting.

To cut, copy, or clear a cell or cell range, follow these steps:

1. Select the cell or cell range, which displays the Edit popover.

2. In the Edit popover, do one of the following:

   - Tap Cut or Copy. If you choose Cut, the data in the cells will become dimmed, and a marquee appears around the selected cell range (the so-called "marching ants"). If you choose Copy, the view of the data within the boundaries doesn't change, but the marquee still appears, clueing you that an operation is in progress.

   - Tap Clear. The data disappears from the selected cell range, and you can skip the rest of these steps.

3. Tap the top left cell where you want to start pasting and tap Paste from the Edit popover. The cut or copied cells appear at the selected location.

▶ **TIP** You can easily move cells to a new location by selecting the cells and dragging them to a different spot on your worksheet. Doing so is the same as cutting and pasting, but moving cells in this way is faster and more practical when you can see both the original location and the destination. If your destination is beyond the screen boundaries, the worksheet will automatically scroll. If you are using an external Bluetooth keyboard, you can also use the familiar command keys (Cmd-X, Cmd-C, Cmd-V) to cut, copy, and paste, respectively.

Entering data

Excel lets you enter data into cells in two ways. You can double-tap to bring up the onscreen keyboard and type directly into the cell, or you can tap once to select the cell and then tap again to place the insertion point into the Formula Bar to enter information. The first method is best when you're entering text or numbers only; the second is better when you are entering formulas, because you can more easily see the whole formula, especially if it is a long one.

Excel for iPad gives you extra help in the data entry department by providing an alternate onscreen numeric keyboard that is available whenever you are typing. To display the alternate keyboard, double-tap in a cell or select the cell and tap in the Formula Bar, which brings up the onscreen keyboard. At the top of the keyboard, tap the 123 switch, and the keyboard changes (11.7).

11.7 Excel's numeric keyboard makes data entry much easier.

Notice how the numeric keyboard contains the extremely useful Tab and arrow keys to help you move around the worksheet. Tapping the Sigma (Σ) key in an empty cell below a column of numbers will insert an AutoSum formula into that cell (11.8). Some of the keys on the numeric keyboard have green marks in their upper-right corners, indicating that if you tap and hold that key, alternate values will appear (11.9). Slide your finger to the alternate value you want.

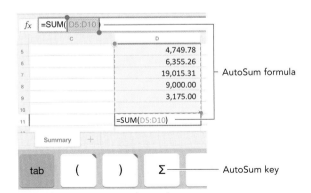

11.8 You can AutoSum a column of numbers with a single keystroke.

11.9 Some keys on the numeric keyboard have alternate values.

Filling data

Excel allows you to easily enter data in a series, and it understands that many things can be a series: numbers, letters, days of the week, a list of months or years, and much more. Excel is quite smart about the way it auto-fills series, allowing you to start with one or two values, and then it fills the remainder of the series correctly. For example, if you enter "Monday" as the start of your series, the auto-fill gives you the rest of the days of the week. But you can also start with two cells containing 2001 and 2003, and the auto-fill continues with odd-numbered years.

To fill a range of cells with a series, follow these steps:

1. Enter an initial value in a cell. If you want Excel to pick up a pattern, enter data in at least two adjacent cells.

2. Tap the cell to select it and bring up the Edit popover (see 11.6).

3. In the Edit popover, tap Fill. Fill arrows appear at the bottom and right edges of the cell (11.10).

4. Drag the fill arrow in the direction you want the series to appear. When you lift your finger, the values appear (11.11).

▶ **TIP** If you're not sure whether or not Excel's AutoFill will work in a particular situation, just try it. The result might surprise you (11.12).

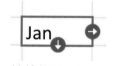

11.10 You can use the fill arrows to fill cells below or to the right.

11.11 All the values after "Jan" were filled in by Excel.

Clear	Fill
Jan	
Feb	
Mar	
Apr	
May	
Jun	
Jul	
Aug	
Sep	
Oct	
Nov	
Dec	

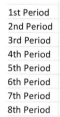

11.12 I typed "1st Period," and Excel's AutoFill did the rest.

1st Period
2nd Period
3rd Period
4th Period
5th Period
6th Period
7th Period
8th Period

Working with Rows and Columns

So far we've talked mostly about cells, but the real building blocks of Excel worksheets are rows and columns. Rows and columns can be inserted, deleted, copied, pasted, and moved. You will probably do these things often, because part of making efficient worksheets is arranging their data logically and coherently.

Selecting rows and columns

To select one or more rows in your worksheet, tap the first row header you want. The row is selected and selection handles appear above and below it (11.13). Extend the selection by dragging one of the selection handles. If you want, you can use the row height handle below the row number to make the selected rows taller or shorter.

4	REVENUES				
5	OPERATING EXPENSES	$65,000.00	$70,962.31	$75,924.67	
6	OPERATING PROFIT	$60,000.00	$64,207.30	$68,857.69	

Cut Copy Insert Above Delete Clear Hide AutoFit

Row height handle   Row selection handles

6	OPERATING PROFIT	$60,000.00	$64,207.30
7	DEPRECIATION	$4,500.00	$4,517.77
8	INTEREST	$2,500.00	$2,745.82

11.13 Tap the row header to select the row (top), then you can drag the selection handles to extend the selection (bottom).

To select one or more columns in your worksheet, tap the first column header you want. The column is selected and selection handles appear at its left and right edges (11.14). You can extend the selection in either direction by dragging one of the selection handles. You can also use the column width handle at the right edge of the column to change the column width.

If you need to cut, copy, delete, clear the values of, or hide a row or column, use the Edit popover that appears when you select the row or column (see 11.13). The AutoFit command in that popover automatically changes the row height or the column width to fit the data contained within.

11.14 Tapping the column header makes its selection handles appear.

Inserting rows and columns

The easiest way to insert a single new row or single new column into a worksheet is to use the Edit popover. Tap a row or column header, then from the resulting Edit popover (see 11.13), choose Insert Above for a row or Insert Left for a column.

Excel also allows you to shift rows, columns, or blocks of cells. Follow these steps:

1. Make a selection. For this example, I have selected a block of cells.

2. On the Home tab of the Ribbon, tap Insert & Delete Cells.

   The Insert & Delete Cells popover appears (11.15). In this figure, all the options are active because I have a block of cells selected. If I had only rows or only columns selected, some options would be dimmed.

11.15 You can shift cells, rows, and columns with this popover.

3. From the popover, choose the operation you want. Your selection will move as you command.

Freezing Panes

One of the frustrations of using a program like Excel on a mobile device is that you simply don't have a lot of screen real estate to work with. When you have worksheets with many rows and columns, and your top row and leftmost column contain headers, it can be awfully frustrating to scroll around and not be able to see the labels for your data. Excel allows you to freeze panes on your screen, allowing you to move around in your data while retaining your view of labels or headers. You have your choice of freezing just the top row, just the first column, or you can freeze rows and columns at the same time at any arbitrary part of your worksheet, allowing you to keep a certain part of your worksheet visible. Remember that you can only freeze a pane on the top or left or top left part of your worksheet. To freeze panes in your worksheet, follow these steps (in this example, I am going to freeze both rows and columns at the same time):

1. Tap to select the cell below and to the right of the row and column you want frozen (11.16).

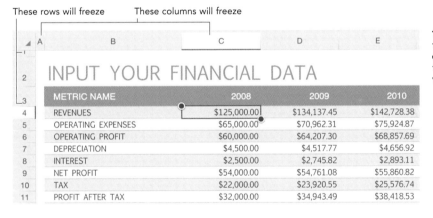

11.16 In this example, the top left portion of the worksheet will freeze, preserving the view of the headers.

2. On the View tab of the Ribbon, tap Freeze Panes. In the resulting pop-over (11.17), tap the option you want.

   Excel adds lines to the worksheet to show you the edges of the panes, and you can scroll without losing sight of your headers (11.18).

▶ **TIP** To unfreeze panes, simply tap Freeze Panes again and uncheck whatever options you set.

11.17 You use this popover to freeze panes.

◢	A	B	E
1			
2		INPUT YOUR F	
3		METRIC NAME	2010
9		NET PROFIT	$55,860.82
10		TAX	$25,576.74
11		PROFIT AFTER TAX	$38,418.53

11.18 You can see the pane lines on the worksheet, and how only parts of the worksheet are scrolling.

CHAPTER 12

Working with Worksheet Data

No matter what you use your worksheets for, it's important that you be able to easily extract meaning from the information and data they contain. Effective formatting is a must because it helps you find what you need at a glance and it makes your data stand out and be easily read.

Besides formatting, functions and formulas are the ways that take the data you've entered in your worksheet and perform calculations on it. You enter raw data, format it as you will, then tell Excel how to crunch the numbers. Excel provides you with a library of hundreds of predefined functions that will meet most of your calculation needs.

In this chapter, you'll see how to format your data to derive easy meaning at a glance, how to build formulas using the formula bar and Excel's built-in functions, and how to make different worksheets work together to provide a useful end result.

Formatting Worksheet Items

Excel gives you the tools to format virtually all the items in your worksheet. When I'm talking about formatting, I'm referring to two different things. The first is the *appearance* of the worksheet: the colors of the cells and their contents, styled cell borders, fonts, font styles, and font sizes, as well as the alignment and orientation of information. The second kind of formatting is *data formatting*, which allows you to tell Excel what kind of information the cells contain. This could be text, numbers, currency values, percentages, dates or times, or more. Data formatting is essential for Excel to calculate your data correctly.

Formatting appearance

As with many other kinds of documents in Microsoft Office, Excel workbooks come with *themes*, which is a combination of preset appearance settings created by Microsoft to work well together and that are part of every workbook template. Even the New Blank Template available in the file manager comes with a theme. You can't edit or apply a different theme to a workbook in Excel for iPad; that ability is reserved for Excel's desktop versions. Instead, you have your choice of many different preset styles that you can apply with just a tap of your finger.

12.1 You can make repeated selections from the Cell Borders popover to get the effect you want.

▶ **TIP** When you're concentrating on formatting your worksheet, you might want to hide parts of Excel's interface to give you more room in which to work. The View tab of the Ribbon allows you to show or hide the formula bar, sheet tabs, headings, and gridlines.

To apply simple styles, use the Home tab of the Ribbon the same way you do in any of the Office programs. First select what you want to format, then choose any combination of the font, font size, bold, italic, or underline.

You can apply borders to a cell or a range of cells. First make your cell selection, then tap Cell Borders from the Home tab of the Ribbon. From the resulting popover (12.1), choose the cell border style you want. You may need to apply border settings multiple times to get the effect that you want.

Excel allows you to set the color of either cell backgrounds or cell contents with adjacent controls on the Home tab of the Ribbon (12.2). Follow these steps:

1. Select the cell or range of cells you want to color.

2. Choose either Cell Fill Color or Cell Content Color.

   The color popover appears (12.3). The popovers for either choice are almost identical; the figure shows the popover for Cell Fill Color.

Cell Content Color

Cell Fill Color

12.2 You can fill cells with color, or color their contents.

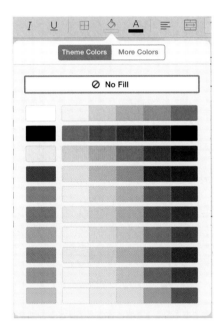

12.3 You get a wide selection of colors in the popover, complementary to the workbook's theme.

3. Tap the color you want, and the change is applied to your worksheet (12.4).

▶ **TIP** You aren't limited to the theme colors Microsoft gives you. In the color popover you can tap More Colors to display a pallet of 10 standard colors, or you can tap Custom Color to display a custom color picker (12.5).

1047.90
1257.48
1467.06
1676.64
1886.22
2095.80
2305.38
2514.96
2724.54
2934.12

12.4 These cells have had their background color changed.

By using the Cell Styles popover, you can easily apply multiple appearance presets in a single operation. When you want to apply more than one format at a time to part of your worksheet, it is easiest to apply a style, because it ensures uniformity. Cell styles are part of the template's theme, and you can't change them. Follow these steps:

1. Select the cell or range of cells you want to style. Don't forget you can select entire rows or columns as well.

2. Tap Cell Styles in the Home tab of the Ribbon.

3. In the resulting popover (12.6), tap the style you want, and the change is applied to your worksheet.

   The Cell Styles popover will have different sets of colors and styles, depending on the underlying workbook template. The different sections of the popover (Good, Bad and Neutral, Data and Model, Titles and Headings, and Themed Cell Styles) and the different style names are suggestions, not requirements. If you want to use the Good style for your totals, go for it.

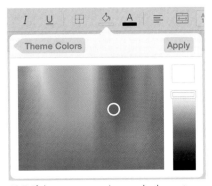

12.5 If the presets aren't enough, the custom color picker is always available.

12.6 Use the Cell Styles popover to apply a wide variety of styles in a single tap.

Formatting number values

Excel lets you specify number formats for any selected cells or ranges. You can choose from many different number formats, and your choices affect the way data is displayed and calculated. It's important to set the number format you want to make sure that your calculations are correct. For example, if you want to calculate the number of days between two dates, Excel understands how to do the calculation by using the Date number format. Excel can often identify an entry in a cell and apply formatting automatically, but it's always best to check.

To apply a number format to a cell or range, follow these steps:

1. Select the cell or range, and then tap Number Formatting on the Home tab of the Ribbon.

2. In the resulting popover (12.7), choose the number format you want. The number format is applied to the selection.

3. (Optional) If the number format you chose has options, you may tap its options button, and the popover changes to display the options (12.8), which of course are different for each kind of number format. Adjust the options as needed.

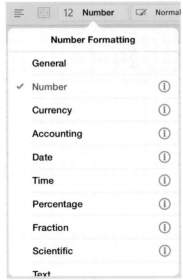

12.7 Choose the number format you need for your selection.

12.8 Some number formats have options, which let you set different number characteristics.

▶ **TIP** Applying some number formats will make the newly formatted values no longer fit in their cells. Excel shows this by replacing the values with #s (12.9). You can fix this by using the column width handle to make the column wider, or you can tap the column header and choose AutoFit from the resulting Edit popover.

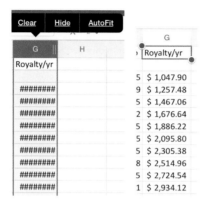

12.9 If cell values are replaced with #s (left), tap AutoFit in the Edit popover to fix the problem (right).

Copying formats

Beside using styles, you can also copy formatting from one spot on your worksheet and paste them to another part. This is especially useful when you have done extensive manual formatting, rather than use the preset styles. Follow these steps:

1. Select the cell from which you want to copy the formatting. The Edit popover appears (12.10).

12.10 You can use the Edit popover to copy and paste formats.

2. In the Edit popover, tap Copy.

3. Select the target cell or cell range to which you want to copy the formatting. The Edit popover reappears.

4. Tap Paste Format, and the target takes on the copied formatting.

Building Formulas

Functions and formulas do the same things. The difference is that functions are built into Excel and provide simpler ways to do complex calculations. You write your own formulas, but you can use Excel's functions in your formulas or on their own. The simplest function in Excel is SUM. This function adds all the numbers in a range of cells and displays the total. A formula using SUM can be written as =SUM(A1:A3). This tells Excel to apply the SUM function to the cell range in parentheses. If you wanted, you could write the same formula like so: =A1+A2+A3. The results of the calculation would be the same, but in the first case you call up Excel's SUM function, and in the second you are simply adding numbers. There's hardly any difference in such a simple example, but with more complex calculations (say, for example, you were adding a column of 100 numbers), you end up saving a lot of time and typing by using functions. When you use functions, you don't need to know what formulas are behind them, because functions encapsulate complex math in easy to use packages.

Functions return calculations based on data in cells or ranges. They use specific values, called *arguments*, in a specific order. Arguments can be numbers, text, or references to individual cells or ranges. These references can be to cells on the worksheet using the function, or to other worksheets in the same workbook (see "Linking Worksheets," later in this chapter).

Functions must be part of formulas, and every function must be entered using specific order, or *syntax*. Going back to the SUM function, here's an example of its syntax as used in a formula:

=SUM(A4, B12, C6:C10)

The equal sign indicates that the worksheet cell contains a formula, as opposed to simply text or a number entered in the cell. Then comes the function name, SUM. This function adds all the values in the arguments contained within the parentheses and returns this sum, which is displayed in the cell containing the formula. Within the parentheses, arguments are separated by commas, and the colon is used to indicate a range of cells, in this case, from cell C6 through cell C10. So in this formula, Excel totals the values in cells A4, B12, and cell range C6 to C10. The result of this calculation is displayed in the cell, and this result can be used elsewhere in other formulas.

Each function has a specific syntax (or to put it another way, its own set of rules) and requires arguments to make calculations. Arguments can be numbers, text, cell references or ranges, or even other functions. The rules for specific functions are beyond the scope of this book, but in general, each function uses different kinds of arguments (you can't add text using the SUM function for example) and each function has a limit to the number of arguments that can handle. You aren't required to memorize or guess how Excel works; you can check the syntax for a function as you are using it. More on that in a moment.

You'll find Excel for iPad's functions on the Formulas tab of the Ribbon (12.11). They are organized in nine categories, as described in **Table 12.1**.

12.11 Use the Formulas tab of the Ribbon to insert the different kinds of functions.

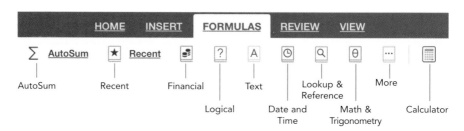

Table 12.1 Excel Function Categories

Category	Description
AutoSum	Attempts to automatically perform calculations on a range of cells near the active cell. You can choose from five common numeric functions.
Recent	Shows a list of recently used functions.
Financial	Makes financial calculations, such as calculating interest and appreciation for loans.
Logical	Allows you to create logical tests of data. Returns true and false values.
Text	Carries out many kinds of operations on text data, such as finding and replacing, substitution, and concatenation.
Date and Time	Performs calculations with dates and times, calculating things such as the number of hours between two times.
Lookup & Reference	Identifies and performs operations on data in tables.
Math & Trigonometry	Returns and calculates a wide variety of mathematical values, such as sines and cosines, returns logarithms, works with scientific notation, and rounds numbers.
More	Contains four more categories of functions: statistical, engineering, info, and database.

When you tap one of the function categories, you get a popover with a list of functions (12.12). Most of these popovers are scrollable, because there are so many functions available. To discover the syntax used by a particular function, tap its info button, and the popover changes to display the syntax and give you a brief description.

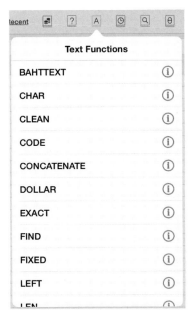

12.12 The Text Functions popover has many text functions (left). Tapping a function's info button shows you the function's syntax and description (right).

Whenever you use a function, it automatically gets added to the Recent popover, which can save you a lot of time, because there are so many functions that it can often take you several minutes just to find the particular function you are looking for. Worksheets tend to use particular functions in multiple cells, so don't forget about Recent. The Recent popover gets reset whenever Excel is fully quit.

Using the Formula Bar

It's possible to type formulas directly into cells, but it is much easier to use the Formula Bar (12.13). Tap the cell where you want to enter a formula, and start typing in the Formula Bar. Every formula begins with an equal sign (=), which tells Excel that the text you are entering is a formula. If a cell or cell range is part of your formula, Excel automatically color codes them with the same colors in both the worksheet and the Formula Bar. To build a formula, you enter elements in the Formula Bar in the appropriate order. In the following simple example, I used an Excel function, COUNTA, to count the number of items in a cell range, then multiplied the result by 25. To walk through the process, follow these steps:

Functions   Formula field   Cancel   Enter

fx =SUM(G3:G12)|

12.13 You'll enter most formulas in the Formula Bar.

1. Select the cell where you want to place the formula, and enter an equal sign in the Formula Bar.

   In this example, I'm using the onscreen keyboard, set to numeric mode. As soon as I typed the equal sign, Excel displayed a Functions popover from the Formula Bar, showing both recently used functions and all other Excel functions (12.14).

12.14 Excel expects you will want to use functions in your formula, and provides a handy popover in the Formula Bar.

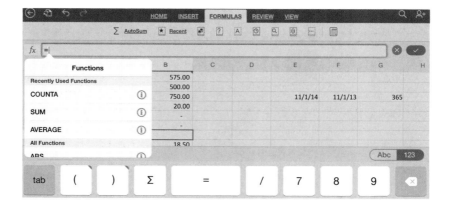

2. In the popover, scroll to the function you want, then tap to select it.

   or

   If you want to insert a cell reference or cell range into the formula, tap or tap and drag in the worksheet to select what you want. Alternatively, you can type the cell reference into the formula.

I chose the COUNTA function, and Excel inserted it into the formula field, highlighting the first placeholder argument I needed to enter for that function (12.15).

3. Type or select a cell or range for the argument, replacing the placeholder. If there are more placeholders that you don't need (as in 12.15), don't use them. Excel will automatically get rid of them as long as they don't contain values or aren't needed for that function.

4. Still in the Formula Bar, tap to the right of the closing parentheses to get out of the function, then type the rest of the formula in the formula field. (12.16).

fx =COUNTA(value1 , value2 , ...)

12.15 Excel inserts functions into the Formula Bar with placeholders for expected values.

fx =COUNTA(A3:A12 , value2 , ...)*25

12.16 The unused gray placeholders will be eliminated when I press Enter.

5. Tap the green checkmark Enter button. The result of the calculation displays in the cell containing the formula.

Linking Worksheets

Excel lets you use data from any location in your workbook in a formula. You can use information from the same worksheet, or you can draw information from other worksheets inside the same workbook. One of the limitations of Excel for iPad is that unlike the desktop versions, it can't access data from other workbooks. A common reason to access data between different worksheets is that you might have the main worksheet in a workbook as a summary worksheet that consolidates information from other, secondary worksheets in the workbook. Linking information between worksheets is easy; follow these steps.

1. Tap the cell in your worksheet where you want to place the results of your calculation.

2. Type =, and if needed, enter the formula you want for the calculation. As part of the formula, when you need to refer to the data from

the other worksheet, tap the sheet tab of the worksheet that contains the data, then tap the cell in that worksheet to which you want to refer (12.17).

16	Accounting	$	150.00
17	Legal	$	300.00
18	Publishing	$	100.00
19	Agents	$	150.00
20	Authors x 3	$	225.00
21			
22	Totals	$	925.00
23			

| Summary | Consults | + |

12.17 Data from the highlighted cell from the secondary Consults worksheet will end up on the Summary worksheet.

3. When you are done with the formula, tap the Enter button in the Formula Bar. The formula shows the *external reference* to the cell in the other worksheet (12.18).

Excel shows external references as the name of the worksheet being referenced, followed by an exclamation point, then followed by the cell reference in the other worksheet.

fx	=Consults!B22	
	A	B
24	iStockPhoto Credits (12)	$ 18.50
25	DBA fee	$ 25.00
26	Professional consultations	$ 925.00
27		
28	**Total**	$ **3,063.50**

12.18 Excel shows the external reference in the Formula Bar.

CHAPTER 13

Building Charts

The cliché that "a picture is worth a thousand words," is often literally true, and in the world of Excel, a chart is often worth a thousand cells. It's not easy to gain meaning from rows and columns of data, but a well-designed chart can make your data understandable in a glance. When it comes to the details, nothing beats the set of numbers, but charts offer a great way to let people quickly grasp the relationship between numbers on your worksheet and help them spot trends. Just by the way, some people call them "charts," some call them "graphs," but they are the same things. Excel calls them charts, so that's what I'm doing, too.

Excel for iPad gives you many tools for creating and working with charts, though those tools are necessarily more limited than the desktop versions. The iPad version relies more on preset styles and layouts, and doesn't give you as much control of the look and content of your charts. Still, you'll find more than enough power to create good-looking charts to communicate your points.

In this chapter, you'll see what kinds of charts are available in Excel for iPad, how to create a chart from worksheet data, and how to apply styles and different layouts to your charts.

Creating Charts

Excel uses two different tabs on the Ribbon to create and work with charts. You'll begin creating any chart on the Insert tab of the Ribbon (13.1). Once the chart has been created, or any time you select a chart on your worksheet, the contextual Chart tab appears in the Ribbon (13.2), which allows you to modify the chart.

13.1 Insert a new chart using the Insert tab of the Ribbon.

13.2 Once your chart has been created, you'll modify it with the Ribbon's contextual Chart tab.

To create a chart, you first need to select the worksheet data you want to visualize. You are generally going to select a group of contiguous cells to be charted, and your original worksheet may not have those data in an easy-to-use form (13.3). It is often better to create a separate worksheet for charting, with only the data you want to chart copied from the original worksheet (13.4).

	A	B	C	D	E	F	G
1	Book topic	Book price	Royalty rate	Net royalty	Books sold/mo	Royalty/ mo	Royalty/yr
2							
3	Swift	$ 4.99	70%	$ 3.49	25	$ 87.33	$ 1,047.90
4	C#	$ 4.99	70%	$ 3.49	30	$ 104.79	$ 1,257.48
5	Java	$ 4.99	70%	$ 3.49	35	$ 122.26	$ 1,467.06
6	C	$ 4.99	70%	$ 3.49	40	$ 139.72	$ 1,676.64
7	Objective C	$ 4.99	70%	$ 3.49	45	$ 157.19	$ 1,886.22
8	Python	$ 4.99	70%	$ 3.49	50	$ 174.65	$ 2,095.80
9	Perl	$ 4.99	70%	$ 3.49	55	$ 192.12	$ 2,305.38
10	Ruby on Rails	$ 4.99	70%	$ 3.49	60	$ 209.58	$ 2,514.96
11	PHP	$ 4.99	70%	$ 3.49	65	$ 227.05	$ 2,724.54
12	JavaScript	$ 4.99	70%	$ 3.49	70	$ 244.51	$ 2,934.12
13							
14	First year income total						$ 19,910.10

13.3 Our original worksheet includes data we don't want to chart (columns B through F).

	A	B
1	Book Topics	
2	Topic	Revenue
3	Swift	$ 1,047.90
4	C#	$ 1,257.48
5	Java	$ 1,467.06
6	C	$ 1,676.64
7	Objective C	$ 1,886.22
8	Python	$ 2,095.80
9	Perl	$ 2,305.38
10	Ruby on Rails	$ 2,514.96
11	PHP	$ 2,724.54
12	JavaScript	$ 2,934.12
13	Total	$ 19,910.10

13.4 Copy just the data we want to chart to a different part of the worksheet.

Excel has a very quick and easy method of creating a chart, called *recommended charts*. To create a recommended chart, follow these steps:

1. In your worksheet, tap and drag to select the data you wish included in the chart, as shown in 13.4.

   If you have worksheet data that includes totals, the totals will often interfere with the visualization of your worksheet data, because each data series is much smaller than its total. So when you make your selection from the worksheet, omit the totals rows or columns, as I did in the figure. This isn't a hard and fast rule; there may be situations in which you want the totals to display in the chart. But if your worksheet has header rows or columns, do select them, because Excel will use them as labels for the chart.

2. On the Insert tab of the Ribbon, tap Recommended.

   Excel does a quick analysis of the selected data and populates the Recommended popover with thumbnails of your selection displayed as chart types that it thinks best show off the data (13.5). This popover is scrollable, so more chart types may be available than you immediately think.

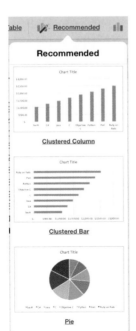

13.5 The Recommended popover gives you Excel's guess for the best chart types for your data.

3. Tap the thumbnail of the chart type you want, and the chart appears in your worksheet (13.6). The Chart tab will also appear in the Ribbon and become active.

13.6 The chart appears in your worksheet, with parts of the worksheet data that made up the chart highlighted and colored.

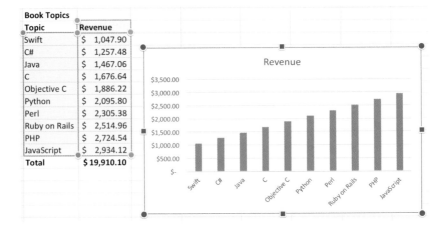

Book Topics	
Topic	Revenue
Swift	$ 1,047.90
C#	$ 1,257.48
Java	$ 1,467.06
C	$ 1,676.64
Objective C	$ 1,886.22
Python	$ 2,095.80
Perl	$ 2,305.38
Ruby on Rails	$ 2,514.96
PHP	$ 2,724.54
JavaScript	$ 2,934.12
Total	**$ 19,910.10**

Excel highlights and color codes the different parts of your selected data to show you what information it used for different parts of the chart. In 13.6, the Revenue label highlighted in red in the worksheet data became the chart title; the book topics highlighted in purple became the names of the data series along the bottom of the chart; and Excel used the values highlighted in blue to create the chart bars.

The chart is "live" and connected to the worksheet data. If you change the values on the worksheet, the chart automatically updates to reflect the new data.

4. (Optional) Once you have created a chart, you can move it to a different spot on the worksheet by tapping and dragging the chart's edge, and you can resize the entire chart by tapping and dragging any of the selection handles.

▶ **TIP** Want to focus on formatting your chart? You can always cut or copy it from the worksheet where it was created and paste it into a new worksheet in your workbook. This allows you to make the chart larger and work with it without the distraction of the worksheet data in the background.

You have many more choices in charts than appear in the Recommended popover, and often you'll know exactly what chart type you want to use to visualize your data. Excel offers 2D and 3D versions of most types of charts. Follow these steps to insert a particular chart type:

1. Select the worksheet data you wish included in the chart.

2. From the Insert tab of the Ribbon, tap Charts, which displays the Charts popover (13.7).

3. Tap the chart type you want, and the popover changes to show the options for the chart type (13.8).

4. Tap to select the chart option you want, and the chart appears in your worksheet (13.9).

▶ **TIP** If you realize the chart isn't what you want, you can change it to a different chart type by tapping Types on the contextual Chart tab of the Ribbon, then choose a different chart type.

5. Many chart types appear in your worksheet with the generic "Chart Title" at the top. To change that, double tap it, then type in the new title.

▶ **TIP** You aren't limited to one chart per data set. You can create multiple charts with different chart types if you like, and have them all appear on the same worksheet, or on different worksheets.

13.7 Use the Charts popover if you know what sort of chart you want to insert.

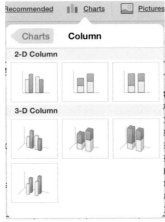

13.8 Each chart type has its own options.

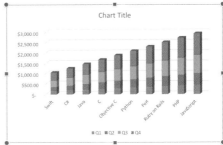

13.9 This is a stacked 3D column chart, with each column made up of the calendar quarters.

Formatting Chart Styles

After you create a chart and it appears in your worksheet, you may or may not be thrilled with the default appearance of the chart. No problem; Excel gives you a way to quickly style the chart with a selection of preset designs, some of which can greatly change and improve the look of your chart. To apply a new chart style, begin by selecting the chart in your worksheet. Then, on the Chart tab of the Ribbon, tap Styles and choose one of the preview thumbnails from the resulting popover (13.10).

13.10 Each chart type has its own set of style presets.

> ▶ **NOTE** Depending on the chart type, you'll see more or less preset designs in the Styles popover. The popover is scrollable, so be sure to check for possibly hidden styles.

Your chart will change, sometimes dramatically (13.11), and if you like the change, go about your work. If the new style isn't quite your cup of tea, immediately tap Undo in the Ribbon, then try again with a different style.

When you choose styles, you want to especially be on the lookout for features that make it easier to visualize your data. For example, some styles include the numeric value of the data (sometimes called *data labels*) in the chart, which might make a column chart with many columns look cluttered, but could be just the ticket for a pie chart (13.12).

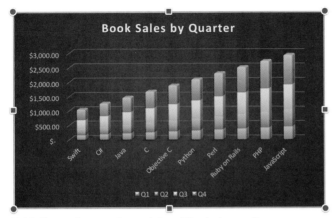

13.11 Chart styles range from subtle to "Hey, look at me!"

13.12 Sometimes data labels help explain small differences in different parts of your chart.

Once you have settled on a chart style you like, you can further customize it by changing the colors used. To do that, select the chart and tap Colors from the Chart tab of the Ribbon. The resulting popover is scrollable and gives you a selection of colors coordinated with the workbook's theme (13.13). The popover has two categories: Colorful, which uses a variety of colors to depict different values in a data series, and Monochromatic, which uses different shades of the same color to depict the data variations. Most of the Monochromatic choices are available in dark-to-light and light-to-dark choices, allowing you to, for example, decide if data is depicted as getting lighter or darker at the end of a bar or column. Tap the color combination you want to apply to your chart (13.14).

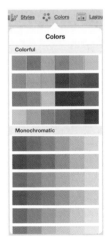

13.13 You can completely recolor your chart using the Colors popover.

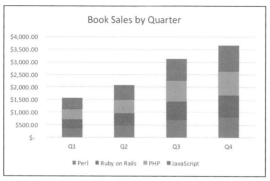
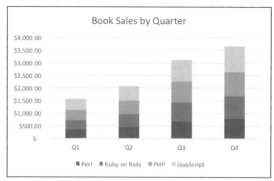

13.14 Here's an example of using the Colorful (left) or Monochromatic (right) color palettes.

Applying Chart Layouts

Excel also allows you to change the way your chart appears with another collection of presets, called *layouts*. Layouts can add information to your chart (such as labels for the different chart axes), or do things like move around where the chart legends appear. You can stack the changes made by chart styles, colors, and layouts to create an almost infinite variety of looks for your charts.

To apply a new layout to a chart, begin by selecting the chart on the worksheet, then tap Layouts in the Chart tab of the Ribbon. The resulting popover gives you thumbnail layouts for the particular chart type you have selected (13.15). Tap a layout to apply it to your chart (13.16).

13.15 Different chart types will offer you differing numbers of layouts.

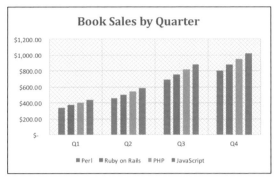
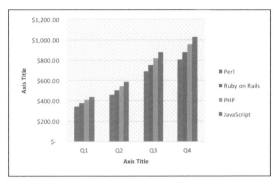

13.16 The original layout (left) loses the chart title and moves the legend to the right edge of the chart (right).

New parts of the chart may appear with the new layout. For example, some layouts include axis titles, as shown in 13.16. You can change them from their generic titles by tapping on the titles to select them, then typing the axis title you want.

Switching Chart Axes

Sometimes the data plotted in a chart isn't being displayed on the axis you want. For example, you might have a worksheet that shows sales for a particular month in successive years for several manufacturers. One way of charting the data would be to chart the data by manufacturer, with its sales performance for each year side-by-side (13.17). But to make it easier to compare how each manufacturer did in successive years, you can switch rows to columns in the chart, and see a different view of the data. Follow these steps:

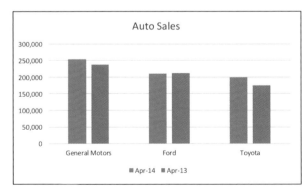

13.17 Viewed this way, you can easily compare each manufacturer's performance year-to-year.

1. Select the chart in your worksheet.

2. On the Chart tab of the Ribbon, tap Switch (13.18).

   The chart changes, allowing you to visualize the data in a whole new way (13.19).

CHART

Switch

13.18 Change the X- and Y-axes of the chart with the Switch icon.

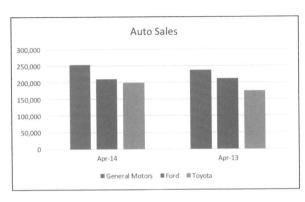

13.19 This visualization makes it easy to compare each manufacturer's sales to its competitors.

3. (Optional) Further format the chart with styles, colors, and layouts until you get the final result you want.

CHAPTER 14

Building Presentations

PowerPoint for iPad, is, in my opinion, the best suited of all the Office apps to the iPad. Though it doesn't have all the bells and whistles you'll find in the desktop versions of PowerPoint, it maintains more than enough power and flexibility to modify existing presentations you created on the desktop, and you can do a pretty fine job of creating new presentations on the road.

Like Word and Excel, you'll get the most out of PowerPoint by combining it with Microsoft's extensive template library, as discussed in Chapter 5. Using templates gives you a big leg up in creating your presentations, whether on the iPad or the desktop.

Probably most of the time, your PowerPoint presentations will begin on PowerPoint for Windows or Mac, be saved to your OneDrive, then be opened in PowerPoint for iPad to make sure that it looks good in the tablet environment and to make last-minute changes.

In this chapter, we'll cover importing presentations from the desktop, with a special concern for modifications you might need to make on the iPad, as well as how to create presentations from scratch in PowerPoint for iPad.

Importing Existing Presentations

Though the iPad is an incredibly useful tool, most people will still find that they can get things done faster and easier with a desktop or notebook computer sporting a hardware-based keyboard and a mouse or trackpad as a pointing device.

The easiest way to get your PowerPoint presentation onto your iPad is to save it into the OneDrive folder on your Mac or Windows machines. The presentation file will be automatically synchronized to the OneDrive cloud storage. Follow these steps to retrieve a PowerPoint presentation from OneDrive on your iPad:

1. Tap the PowerPoint icon on your iPad.

    By default, PowerPoint launches to the Open tab of the file manager, set to your OneDrive (14.1).

14.1 Begin importing PowerPoint presentations from your OneDrive using the Open tab of PowerPoint's file manager.

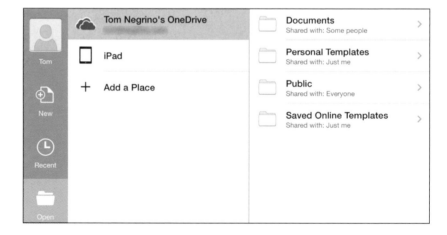

2. In the file manager, tap the folder that contains your presentation.

3. Tap the icon for your presentation in the rightmost column. It downloads from OneDrive and appears in PowerPoint (14.2).

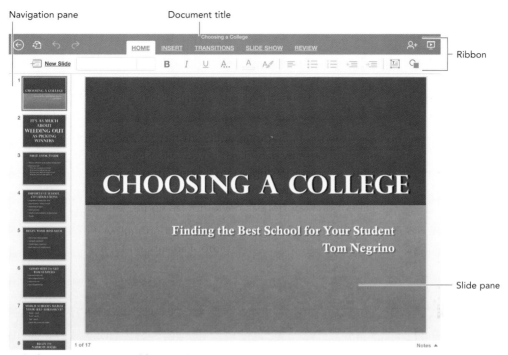

Navigation pane   Document title   Ribbon   Slide pane

14.2 The presentation, opened from OneDrive.

Watch for pitfalls

Because not all the features that are available in the Windows or Mac versions of PowerPoint are present in PowerPoint for iPad (see the "PowerPoint for iPad Limitations" sidebar), it's important to go through all the slides in your PowerPoint deck well before the date of your presentation. There are a variety of things you need to be looking for, but you need to make sure the presentation experience you want for your audience will be available when you give your presentation. By reviewing your presentation on the iPad, you can make sure that things on your slides look as you expect, tweaking them if necessary.

The most likely culprits for poor fidelity between a PowerPoint presentation on a computer and your iPad are fonts. There are many more fonts available for computers than exist on the iPad. The problems you can have when fonts from one platform are remapped onto fonts from another platform is the possibility that your slide text could end up being misaligned, text could wrap in places you didn't anticipate, or otherwise mess up the designs of your slides. For PowerPoint for iPad, you have three classes of fonts available to you from the font menu in the Ribbon:

- **Theme Fonts** are fonts that are part of the PowerPoint presentation theme, that is, the design that makes up the PowerPoint template from which the presentation was created. A set of theme fonts are two or more fonts that are designed to work well with a particular theme. Many of the standard fonts that Microsoft uses for PowerPoint themes are built into the PowerPoint app, allowing you to use those fonts on the iPad.

- **Office Compatible Fonts** are fonts that are widely used in Microsoft products, and are often shipped with or embedded in those products. This set of fonts includes the theme fonts used by the last several versions of PowerPoint for Windows and Mac, so if you stick to using fonts from this set, you should experience excellent fidelity between platforms. You can discover more information about fonts and Microsoft products at Microsoft's typography site: www.microsoft.com/typography/fonts.

- **iOS Fonts** are fonts that Apple supplies with iOS, the iPad operating system. You can see examples of these fonts as used on both the iPhone and iPad at http://iosfonts.com.

Besides font problems, you may also have difficulty with media files embedded in your PowerPoint presentations. PowerPoint for iPad, at press time, could not play either video or audio files embedded on PowerPoint slides.

When you are preparing your PowerPoint presentation on a Mac or Windows machine, for image files it's best to stick with PNG or JPG format. Other formats, notably TIF, tend to produce files that are large in size and often incompatible. Image files are embedded inside PowerPoint presentation files, so you should limit their file size while maintaining the image quality you need. Happily, since you will be presenting on a screen, you don't need the kind of high resolution images required for print applications.

PowerPoint for iPad Limitations

You may be used to some features that are available in the Windows or Mac versions of PowerPoint, but find that they are missing on PowerPoint for iPad. Here is a list of some of the features that you won't find in the mobile version.

- Slide animations: Can play animations created on Windows or Mac, but can't create, change, or remove slide animations.

- Slide transitions: Can add, change, and remove slide transitions from other platforms, but some transition types may not be available. Also, slide transitions may be applied to one slide or all slides, but not multiple slides in a single action.

- Charts: Cannot create charts, but can copy and paste from Excel for iPad. Some modification in PowerPoint possible.

- Video clips: Cannot play, add, or change video clips within slides. You can, however, select and remove a video clip.

- Audio clips: Cannot play, add, or change audio clips within slides. You can, however, select and remove an audio clip.

- Smart Art: Can display and remove, and can change text styles, but cannot add or change components of SmartArt diagrams.

- Comments: Can display, but cannot add, remove, or change slide comments.

Fix problems

You don't always have control over the history of your presentation file. For example, it could have started out life as an Apple Keynote file that was then later converted to PowerPoint. In a case like that, the chances are excellent that there will be font issues you will want to clean up. For example, in the presentation file shown in **14.3**, the file was originally created in Keynote on the Mac, and used fonts and font sizes that would have been correctly translated to Keynote on the iPad, but formatting was lost in translation. The font, Georgia, came through just fine, but the font size appeared in PowerPoint as 63.36 points instead of 64 point. To check for and fix font problems in your PowerPoint presentations, follow these steps:

14.3 An odd number in the Font Size menu alerts you to a problem that should be fixed.

1. Open the presentation file in PowerPoint.

2. Tap the first slide in the navigation pane.

3. Tap each of the text boxes on the slide to select it, looking for problems in the Font and Font Size menus in the Ribbon. You should also perform a visual inspection of the text on the slide. If you see nothing wrong with the slide, tap the next slide in the navigation pane, and repeat the process until you are done with the presentation.

▶ **TIP** If tapping on a text box accidentally moves it, tap the Undo button in the Ribbon to fix your mistake.

4. If you see a problem with the Font or Font Size, tap that control in the Ribbon.

    The popover you selected appears (14.4).

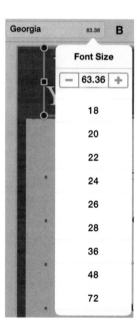

14.4 Tap the Plus button in the Font Size popover to increase the font size to the next integer.

5. Use the controls in the popover to fix the problem.

    For example, in 14.4, tapping the plus button in the Font Size popover changed the font size to the desired value of 64 points.

6. Tap elsewhere on the screen to dismiss the popover, then continue your inspection of the presentation.

Similarly, tap to select any other items on the slides that may not have translated well in its journey to PowerPoint for iPad, and edit the item as needed. Some techniques for editing text and images will be covered in Chapter 15.

Creating Presentations on iPad

You may find it a little easier to start a presentation on a computer, but you'll find that you can create perfectly useful and compelling presentations using PowerPoint for iPad. I do strongly recommend that you invest in an external Bluetooth keyboard, because entering slide text using the onscreen keyboard, with its tendency to cover up the slide text you are typing, can be frustrating.

To create a presentation on PowerPoint for iPad, follow these steps:

1. From PowerPoint's file manager, tap New.

   PowerPoint's built-in templates appear; tap a template.

   or

   To start with a template from another source, follow the instructions in Chapter 5.

   The new PowerPoint document appears, with the first slide already created for you, set to the Title Slide slide master (**14.5**).

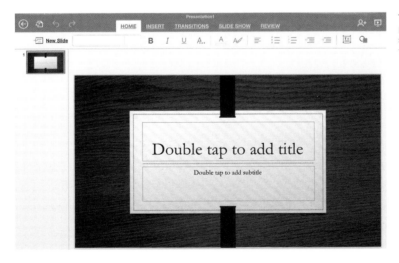

14.5 By default, new presentations always start with a Title Slide formatted slide.

2. Double-tap in the Title box, then type in the title of your presentation.

3. Tap New Slide in the Ribbon.

4. In the New Slide popover (14.6), tap on the slide master you want for the next slide.

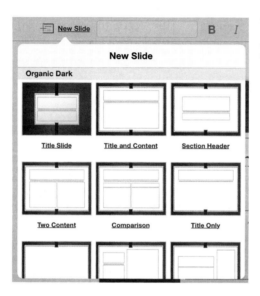

14.6 Use the New Slide popover to create your new slide type.

5. As needed, double-tap in the slide pane to enter text in the text place-holder boxes (14.7), or use the Insert tab in the Ribbon to add images to your presentation (adding images will be covered in Chapter 15).

You can also tap to select a text box to modify its contents.

14.7 After adding a few slides, you can adjust the look of text boxes by tapping them, then choosing a control from the Ribbon.

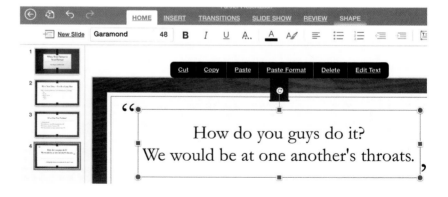

CHAPTER 15

Working with Slides

A PowerPoint document contains all the items that make up your presentation including text, images, pre-drawn graphics (which PowerPoint calls *shapes*), and, if you choose to include them, the animations of slide objects and animated transitions between slides.

In this chapter, you'll learn how to modify entire slides in Power-Point for iPad, how to style text on your slides, how to insert tables and images, and how to insert and work with shapes to help get your presentation's message across better.

Modifying Slides

When you start PowerPoint, the app assumes that you want to resume what you were doing when you last left the program. So, if you were editing a presentation, you'll go back to the same slide within that presentation.

Changing slide order

There are two ways to change the order of the slides in your presentation. You can cut a slide in the navigation pane and paste it elsewhere, or you can tap and drag the slide up or down in the slide list.

To move a slide by cutting and pasting, follow these steps:

1. In the navigation pane, slow double-tap the slide you want to move.

    The Edit popover appears (15.1).

15.1 The Edit popover with a slide selected in the navigation pane. This slide is about to be cut to the clipboard.

2. Tap Cut in the Edit popover, which cuts the slide to the Clipboard.

3. Slow double-tap the slide directly above where you want the slide destination to be (15.2).

15.2 The Edit popover appears again when you are ready to paste the slide to its new location.

4. Tap Paste in the Edit popover.

    The slide is pasted into its new location (15.3).

> **TIP** If you are using an external Bluetooth keyboard, you can't use the usual command keys (Cmd-X, Cmd-C, Cmd-V) to move slides in the navigation pane. Those command keys do work for Clipboard operations in PowerPoint, but they only work for text in text boxes.

To move a slide by dragging it in the navigation pane, tap and hold a slide until its slide number disappears in the navigation pane, then drag it up or down in the list (15.4).

15.3 The moved slide appears below the previously selected slide.

15.4 The dimmed slide is in the process of being moved to above slide 3.

Duplicating slides

Why might you want to duplicate a slide? The most common reason is that you have added some custom elements to a slide—such as a graphic or a custom text box—that you want to appear on a few slides, and you don't want to have to re-create them again and again.

To duplicate a slide, follow these steps:

1. Slow double-tap the slide you want to duplicate, bringing up the Edit popover.

2. Tap Duplicate in the Edit popover.

A copy of the slide is created directly below the existing slide in the navigation pane.

▶ **TIP** Of course, you can also duplicate a slide by copying and pasting it.

Hiding slides

There are times when you have your presentation ready to go, and you arrive at the venue and realize that you don't want to show some of the slides in your presentation. Perhaps your company's product line has just been changed, and you need to skip the slide that shows a product that has been discontinued.

Hidden slides remain in your presentation, but PowerPoint skips over them when you present the show.

To hide a slide, follow these steps:

1. Slow double-tap the slide you want to hide, bringing up the Edit popover.

2. Tap Hide in the Edit popover.

The slide dims in the navigation pane, and the universal icon for "No" is overlayed upon it (15.5).

To show the slide again, select the hidden slide and tap Unhide in the Edit popover.

15.5 The dimmed slide is hidden, and will not appear during the presentation.

Deleting slides

To delete a slide, follow these steps:

1. In the navigation pane, slow double-tap the slide you want to delete, bringing up the Edit popover.

2. Tap Delete in the Edit popover.

   The slide disappears from the navigation pane.

Working with Text

In Chapter 14, you saw how to enter text in the text placeholders on slides. But there's a lot more to be done with text than simply typing it on a slide. Text will often need to be styled in order to underline your message. You might want to add your own text boxes to a slide, if the supplied text placeholders don't suit your fancy.

Styling text

One of the benefits of PowerPoint's many templates is that much of the work of styling is done for you. In many cases, you won't have any need to style slide text, even though you have a fairly complete style toolbox available to you. But when you do need to style text, you have the tools in the Home tab of the Ribbon available to you (15.6).

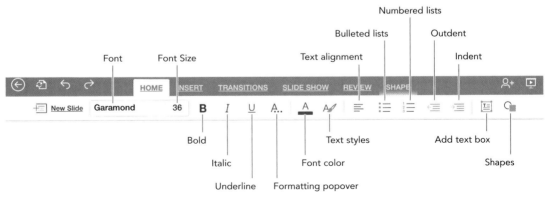

15.6 You'll do most of your text styling using the tools in the Home tab of the Ribbon.

When you have entered text into a text placeholder, you can apply styles to the entire text box, or to selected text within the text box, or you can mix both approaches. If you tap a text box once, it becomes selected, as indicated by the selection handles around the whole box (15.7). Besides the usual selection handles, PowerPoint also includes a rotation handle for every text box that allows you to slant the text at any angle.

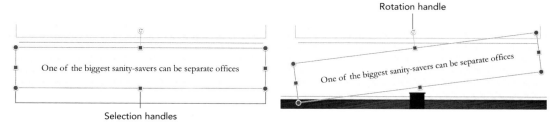

15.7 You can resize a text box with the selection handles (left), and you can rotate the text using the rotation handle (right).

Making style changes to a selected box using the Ribbon will apply those changes to the entire contents of the text box. Follow these steps:

1. In the slide area, tap to select a text box.

   Selection handles appear around the box.

2. Use the controls in the Ribbon to make your desired changes to the contents of the text box.

   In this example, I made the text bold and changed its color (15.8).

15.8 Use the text controls in the Ribbon to take regular text (left) and style it (right).

You can also style some of the text inside a text box differently. Follow these steps:

1. Double-tap on a word inside a text box to select the word (15.9).

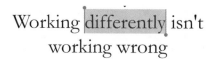

15.9 You can select a word inside a text box by double tapping it.

2. (Optional) Drag the word selection handles to grow or shrink your text selection as needed.

3. Use the controls in the Ribbon to make your desired changes to the contents of the text box.

   In this example, I italicized the text in two places to emphasize my point (15.10).

Working *differently* isn't working *wrong*

15.10 Each word was italicized separately.

PowerPoint also has other styling options in popovers on the Ribbon. The Formatting popover (15.11) allows you to add strikethrough, subscript, and superscript to text, as well as a handy way to clear all formatting. And the Alignment popover (not shown) allows you to align text horizontally left, center, right, or justified, as well as to the top, middle, or bottom of its text box. You can also choose to rotate text within the text box or display text in columns within the text box.

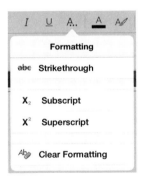

15.11 The Formatting popover gives you additional text formatting abilities, and also allows you to clear formatting altogether.

Copying styles

Sometimes, rather than recreating a set of styles from scratch, it's better to do the job once and then copy the formatting to another text box. When you copy styles, PowerPoint replicates the whole set of styles from the source, including the font, size, text color, and so on, to the target text. The following steps outline the process.

1. In the slide area, tap to select the text box from which you want to copy the styles, also bringing up the Edit popover (15.12).

15.12 Begin copying a style by copying the source text.

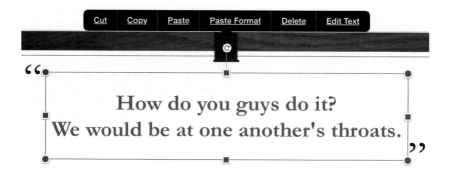

2. In the Edit popover, tap Copy.

3. Select the target text to which you want to copy the styles, which makes the Edit popover appear for that text box.

4. Tap Paste Format.

   The targeted text takes on the styles of the source text (15.13).

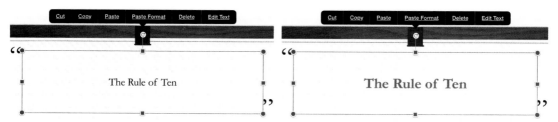

15.13 Select the destination for the copied style (left), then use Paste Format to complete the job (right).

Inserting text boxes

Besides the text placeholders that come with most slides, you can also add your own freestanding text boxes to slides. You can use these whenever you need extra text on a slide. For example, you can use a text box as a picture caption (15.14). Follow these steps to add a freestanding text box:

15.14 By adding my own text box, I was able to achieve the emotional effect I wanted.

1. On the slide where you want to add the text box, tap the Text Box button on the Ribbon.

   A text box appears in the center of the slide.

2. To add text to the box, double-tap inside the box, then type your text.

3. Drag the text box to where you want to position it on the slide.

   As you drag the text box, PowerPoint will show you alignment guides to help you line the text up easily.

▶ **NOTE** Oddly, PowerPoint for iPad does not allow you to find and replace text on slides the way you can with Word documents or Excel worksheets. You can certainly do that with PowerPoint for Windows or Mac, so perhaps it's a feature that will be added to the iPad version sooner or later.

Adding Tables

In presentations, you'll often find it useful to portray data in tables. A table's rows and columns make it easy to present complex information in a simple way. Examples of such data would be financial results, a performance comparison of two or more products, or sometimes even a simple list.

Tables consist of rows and columns. *Rows* are the horizontal divisions of the table; *columns* are the vertical divisions. A row and a column intersect to form a *cell*, which is where you put the contents of a table. You can put text, but not graphics, into a cell.

When you add a table to a slide, PowerPoint automatically creates a table with three rows and three columns. Of these, the top row is the *header row*. You can also format the left column as the *header column*. A header row or column is formatted differently from the rest of the table to highlight the information in the headers. You usually put labels in the header row and column, to help people more easily understand your table.

PowerPoint gives you extensive tools to create and format tables; more, in fact, than I have room to discuss here. I'll walk you through creating and applying basic formatting to a table, then set you free to do your own experimentation.

To create a table, follow these steps:

1. In the navigation pane, tap the slide on which you want to create a table.

2. In the Ribbon, tap the Insert tab, which now displays the Insert tab's contents (15.15).

15.15 Begin adding a table on the Insert tab of the Ribbon.

3. Tap Table.

   The default table appears on the slide, with the table selected, and a new contextual tab, Table, appears in the Ribbon, with tools especially meant for working with tables (15.16).

15.16 The default table appears, as does the contextual Table tab in the Ribbon.

In this example, I wanted a table with five rows and five columns, so I used the Insert popover in the Ribbon to add rows and columns, and the Style Options popover to specify the first column as a header column. Your needs will probably be different.

4. Drag the table's selection handles to resize the table as you prefer on the slide.

5. Double-tap in a cell to enter text.

   To style the text in the cell, double-tap the text to select it, then use the text tools on the Ribbon's Home tab.

6. When you have finished with the table, tap elsewhere on the slide to deselect the table (15.17).

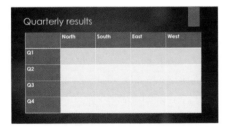

15.17 The finished table is formatted the way I want.

▶ **TIP** If you spend a lot of time formatting a table to have it look just the way you want, before you fill it with data, copy and paste the table into a slide in the presentation that you plan to keep hidden. When you need to update the presentation, you can unhide the slide, copy the table again, and use the formatted slide in your updated slide deck without needing to repeat all that formatting.

Adding Images

The text on your slides will usually carry the weight of your presentation, but the content can be greatly enhanced by the look of your slideshow. Much of that look is provided by the template you select for your presentation. But graphics on the slide can also add visual interest to a professional looking presentation, and often they contribute a significant part of the content of the presentation, as well.

PowerPoint for iPad allows you to add pictures from your photo library to your presentations. Not only do you have access to the photos that are on your iPad, but you also have access to the Photo Stream from iCloud, and depending on the photo software you use and their settings, you may also have access to all the photos contained in Apple's iPhoto or Aperture.

▶ **TIP** If you plan to give a lot of presentations that include photographs using PowerPoint for iPad, you are much better off creating your presentation on PowerPoint for Mac or Windows, then transferring it to the iPad, because the desktop versions of PowerPoint have many more templates that are much better suited for photographs than the built-in templates in PowerPoint for iPad, which generally only have one or two slide masters with photo placeholders. See Chapter 5 for more information about using templates. In the examples in this section, I've used only the built-in templates for PowerPoint for iPad.

To add images to your presentations, follow these steps:

1. Tap the Insert tab in the Ribbon.

2. Tap New Slide, then from the New Slide popover, choose one of the slide Masters that includes a photo placeholder (15.18).

3. On the Insert tab, tap Pictures.

    The Photos popover appears, displaying the photo albums that are available to you (15.19).

15.18 I'm choosing the Picture with Caption slide master, because it contains a photo placeholder.

Photo placeholder

15.19 Choose the photo albums you want from the Photos popover.

4. Tap the photo album that contains the picture you want, scroll the photo album as needed, then tap the picture you want to insert.

The picture appears on the slide, resized to fit the photo placeholder (15.20). PowerPoint also switches to the contextual Picture tab of the Ribbon, allowing you to add styles, shadows, and reflection effects to the picture.

15.20 The inserted picture is resized to fit the photo placeholder, and the contextual Picture tab appears in the Ribbon.

▶ **TIP** One of the drawback in dealing with pictures on PowerPoint for iPad is that you can resize pictures, but you can't re-color, crop or mask them. So if you want to make any serious modifications to an image, make sure that you add one of the many image editing apps to your iPad before you head out on the road.

Creating Shapes

PowerPoint's shapes are vector graphics that can be scaled and manipulated with no loss of resolution. There is a fairly extensive library of shapes, and you can use them to create diagrams on your slides. There are several different collections of shapes: Lines, Rectangles, Basic Shapes, Block Arrows, the Equation Shapes, Flowchart Shapes, Stars and Banners, and Callouts. You can use any of these to add interest or spice up your slides. To add a shape to your slide, follow these steps:

1. In the navigation pane, tap on the slide to which you want to add the shape.

2. Tap the Insert tab in the Ribbon.

3. Tap Shapes.

   The Shapes popover appears, displaying the categories of shapes that are available to you (15.21).

4. Scroll and you find the shape that you want, then tap it.

   The shape appears on the slide. PowerPoint also switches to the contextual Shape tab of the Ribbon, allowing you to add styles, fills, and change the line used by the shape.

5. (Optional) If you want to add text inside the shape, double tap inside the shape, then enter the text, using the controls on the Home tab of the Ribbon to style the text (15.22).

▶ **NOTE** PowerPoint for iPad does not have the ability to create the SmartArt diagrams that you may be familiar with from the Windows or Mac versions of PowerPoint. It can, however, use those diagrams if they are part of an imported presentation.

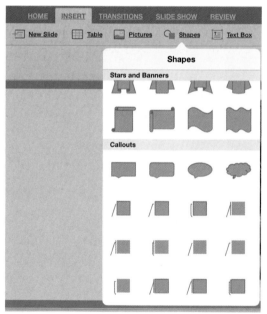

15.21 You can choose from many categories of premade shapes.

15.22 The callout shape was resized, and text added with a typical feline complaint.

CHAPTER 16

Adding Transitions and Presenting

One of the final things you want to add to your presentation are the transitions between slides. They allow you to add motion and visual appeal to your slideshow. *Slide transitions* are animated effects that occur when you switch from one slide to another. *Slide animations* are animations that occur within the body of a slide. In this book, we don't have to worry much about slide animations, because although PowerPoint for iPad can play slide animations that were created on PowerPoint for Windows or Mac, PowerPoint for iPad doesn't have the ability to add, remove, or change slide animations. On the other hand, PowerPoint for iPad has no problems working with slide transitions, and we'll be covering those in detail.

After you put the finishing touches on your presentation, you need to give it. In this chapter, I'll give you some of my favorite tips that I've picked up in more than 20 years of giving presentations, and you'll see what you need in terms of hardware to give the presentation from your iPad.

Add Slide Transitions

Whenever I create a presentation, no matter what software I'm using, I always leave adding animations of any sort as my final task. I believe, backed up by years of experience, that it's easy to become seduced by the flashy animation tools you get with presentation software like PowerPoint, and the animations tend to distract you from what's really important: the message you are presenting. At one time or another, we've all seen Power-Point presentations with enough animation to induce motion sickness, but that essentially had little to say. Don't be one of those presenters.

As mentioned in the introduction to this chapter, PowerPoint for iPad can't add or modify slide animations, though it can play them if they were added to the presentation using PowerPoint for Windows or Mac. We'll talk more about checking out slide animations on PowerPoint for iPad in "Preflight Your Show," later in this chapter.

Slide transitions, however, are a different matter, and they can be added or changed on PowerPoint for iPad. Follow these steps to apply a transition to a particular slide:

1. In PowerPoint for iPad, open your presentation.

2. Tap the Transitions tab.

   The Transition tab appears, with its three controls: Transition Effect, Effect Options, and Apply To All Slides (16.1).

16.1 You add slide transitions on the Transitions tab.

   Notice that an icon of the current slide transition appears next to each of the three controls. Because there is currently no transition effect applied to the selected slide, the Effect Options control is dimmed.

3. In the navigation pane, tap to select the slide to which you want to add or change a transition. This will be the transition to the slide from the previous slide, if any.

You can tell the slide is selected because a red border appears around it (16.2).

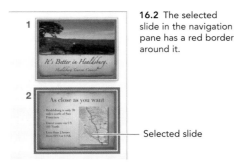

16.2 The selected slide in the navigation pane has a red border around it.

Selected slide

4. To add or change the slide transition, tap Transition Effect in the toolbar.

The Transition To This Slide popover appears (16.3). This popover is scrollable, and groups the available transition effects into Subtle, Exciting, and Dynamic Content. Subtle and Exciting transitions apply to the entire slide. The Dynamic Content transitions apply their animations to the individual text and image boxes within the slide itself, in effect animating the contents of the slide while leaving the background apparently unchanged.

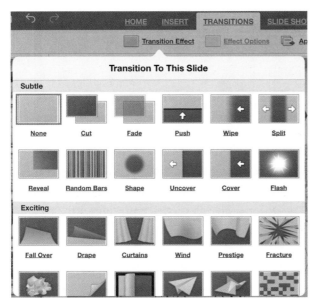

16.3 You'll find many transitions, with varying amounts of visual taste, in the Transition To This Slide popover.

5. If necessary, scroll through the popover to find the transition effect you want, then tap the effect to select it.

The popover disappears and the icon corresponding to the transition you selected appears next to the controls in the toolbar (16.4).

16.4 Once you pick a transition, its icon appears in the toolbar.

6. (Optional) You have the option to allow the transition to happen smoothly, or to have the screen dip briefly to black before the transition triggers. If you want to set this option, tap Effect Options in the toolbar.

The Effect Options popover appears; tap to choose the effect option you want.

7. (Optional) If you like (and in fact, it's often recommended), you can use the same transition effect between all of the slides in your slideshow. Since the slide for which you set the transition effect is still selected, to add that same transition effect to the rest of the slides in your presentation, tap Apply To All Slides in the toolbar.

PowerPoint briefly displays an alert letting you know the transition has been applied to all the slides, and stars appear next to all the slide thumbnails in the navigation pane, indicating that the slide uses a transition.

Preflight Your Show

Preflighting your show means that you should, very carefully, go through the entire presentation, slide by slide, looking for any mistakes. After you build and live with a presentation for hours, days, or even weeks, it's amazing how often you can become desensitized to spelling or grammar mistakes in your slide text, or sometimes even things like using the wrong image on a particular slide.

In fact, this is a great time to enlist the help of a friend or coworker to help you catch mistakes. Use one of the sharing techniques, as discussed in

"Sharing Documents" in Chapter 4, to share a copy of your presentation with a friend. You will be surprised (and perhaps even a bit chagrined) at how often your friend catches a mistake in your presentation.

You should preflight your show in two ways. First, go through every slide in your presentation in editing mode, by simply tapping on each slide in turn in the navigation pane.

▶   **TIP** One trick I found that works surprisingly well is to shrink the slide a bit in the slide pane. Simply pinch in the slide pane to shrink the view of the slide down to about 85% (16.5). For some reason no doubt understood by neuroscientists, this allows you to look at the slide with a fresh view, yet still keeps the slide large enough for you to easily spot mistakes.

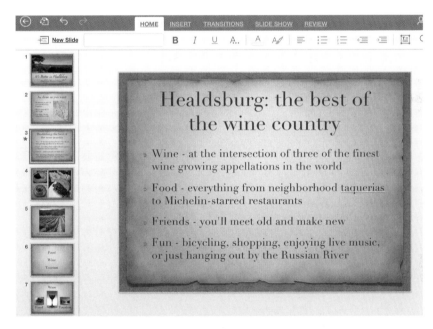

16.5 Shrinking a slide down in the slide pane can make it easier to notice any errors on the slide.

The second way to preflight your show is to enter presentation mode in PowerPoint for iPad and either review the presentation slide by slide or to simply practice your presentation out loud. I recommend the latter approach, because practicing the presentation out loud will often spark ideas of ways to tighten up your presentation. Start by tapping the Begin Slide Show button in the toolbar (16.6), then swipe to change slides.

Share   Begin Slide Show

16.6 Tap the Begin Slideshow button in the toolbar to begin practicing your presentation.

▶ **TIP** While practicing your presentation out loud, try not to stop, and be sure to time your presentation. It's much better to find out your presentation is too long before you perform it to an audience. In the same way, if your presentation is running short, it's better to find out before you're in front of a bunch of expectant faces.

Give the Presentation

The funny thing about presentations is that you went to work creating your presentation and make it look good, and when you're done the real job hasn't even started yet; you still have to give the presentation. For some people, giving a presentation (and public speaking in general) ranks in popularity just this side of dental surgery. Other folks like nothing better than standing in front of an audience. Most of us, however, fall somewhere between those extremes.

Preparing to present

The more presentations you give, the better a speaker you'll be. The key to giving a good presentation is to be prepared, pay attention to the details, and get plenty of practice. Here are some tips that can help your overall presentation be a successful one.

- Unfortunately, things do go wrong; your iPad could die before you give your show, or it could have video problems with the venue's projectors. Make sure you keep a backup copy of your presentation file on something other than your iPad. I prepare two backup copies of important presentations. One of them is on my iPhone, downloaded from OneDrive while I still have a Wi-Fi connection, and the other is on a USB flash drive. That way, if I get to the venue and have hardware troubles, I can almost always borrow a computer with Microsoft Office, load my PowerPoint presentation, and go on with the show.

- If you can, get to the presentation venue a little early. Sit or stand where you will be when you're speaking, and make sure that your seating (or the podium) is adjusted the way you want it. Take a moment to adjust the microphone and work with the venue's AV technician to get the audio levels right before the audience arrives. Make sure you have a spot to place a cup or bottle of water. Getting comfortable with the physical space and the facilities helps a lot.

- Concentrate on your message, not on the audience. If you focus on what you're saying, you will distract yourself from being nervous.

- If you are nervous, *never* apologize for it. Except in extreme cases, most audiences don't notice that speakers are nervous, and it doesn't help your case to point it out. Confidence—even if you're faking it—goes a long way.

- Always keep in mind that your audience *wants* you to succeed. People don't go to a presentation thinking, "I sure hope this person gives a lousy talk and wastes my time." They want to get something out of your presentation as much as you do.

- Never read your slides aloud word for word. Your slides should be signposts and reminders of what you want to say. Using your slides as your teleprompter is another way to lose audience interest.

Making the hardware connection

To get the presentation from your iPad up onto a big screen, you can choose a wired or wireless solution. You will either plug your iPad directly into a video cable leading to a video projector or large monitor, or you will mirror your iPad's screen via AirPlay to the display device.

► **TIP** One of the most important things you can do well before a presentation is find out what sort of video connection the venue is going to use to project your screen. It's a crucial bit of information, especially if you are presenting directly from your iPad (if you were to be presenting from a Mac or a Windows notebook, you would have considerably more flexibility).

Video connections used for monitors and projectors used for presentations come in two flavors:

- **Analog** connections almost always mean a VGA connector that feeds directly into a projector. These are becoming increasingly rare at conference venues.

- **Digital** connections mean either an HDMI connection or a DVI connection. These are the most likely connections you will find, though you might want to carry your own HDMI-to-DVI female video adapter along with you, just to make sure you can handle either possibility.

Using a direct connection

All current iPads and other iOS devices use the Lightning connector as their main hardware connection. Unfortunately, the Lightning connector means that you are limited to one of two video adapters, both made by Apple and both expensive ($50 each in the United States). The Lightning Digital AV Adapter has a male Lightning connector that plugs into your iPad at one end of a short cable and a HDMI and pass-through Lightning connector at the other end. This adapter supports both video and audio. Its analog video counterpart, the Lightning to VGA Adapter, supports video only (no surprise there, as VGA has always been a video-only standard).

Once you get to your presentation venue, work with their AV technician to connect your iPad to their video wiring. You will have to turn on video mirroring, as discussed next. The negative part of using a direct wired connection is that once you are presenting, you are, literally, tethered in one spot by the video cable.

Using an Apple TV and AirPlay

A second, and in my opinion better way to present from your iOS device is to use the $99 Apple TV. The hardware investment is greater (unless you needed to purchase both the Lightning video adapters, in which case it is the same), but you gain more flexibility. The Apple TV is a set top box that provides better video quality than the Lightning adapters, supports audio, and of course also allows you to stream iTunes content, as well as access other services such as Netflix, Major League Baseball, and YouTube. Chances are when you are not doing presentations the Lightning video adapters will be sitting idle in your bag, whereas you can use the Apple TV for home entertainment. Best of all from a presenting standpoint, it uses a Wi-Fi connection between the iPad and the Apple TV, so you are not tied down to one spot while giving your presentation.

One possible drawback is that the Apple TV only has an HDMI output, so you are limited to using it in venues that can accept digital video, unless you also purchase a HDMI to VGA adapter.

Turning on video mirroring

Whether you are using a direct video connection or are streaming video from your iPad wirelessly, you will need to turn on video mirroring on the iPad. Here's how to do that (using iOS 7; though iOS 8 has been announced when I wrote this, it was not yet available). Follow these steps:

1. On your iPad or other iOS device, swipe up from the bottom of the screen.

   The iOS Control Center appears (16.7).

16.7 Begin turning on AirPlay video mirroring in the iOS Control Center.

2. Tap AirPlay.

   The AirPlay sheet appears with a list of devices on the local Wi-Fi network that can accept AirPlay. This could include locally connected monitors, an Apple TV, or even a Mac or Windows computer running AirPlay receiver software.

3. Tap the device you want to use for video streaming. If it isn't already turned on, turn on Mirroring (16.8).

16.8 Remember to flip the Mirroring switch in the AirPlay popover so your video goes to the selected device.

The video (and audio, if supported) output of your iOS device appears on the screen of the external device.

Control the Presentation

Now the presentation and the projector are ready to go in the audience has arrived, it's time to get your presentation going. During the presentation, you can control your show with the iPad's screen. You can also mark up the screen during the presentation with an onscreen pencil or marker.

Playing the presentation

To play your presentation on an external projector or monitor, follow these steps:

1. In the navigation pane, tap to select the first slide in the presentation.

   Of course, if you don't want to start at the first slide, you can select the slide you do want to start on.

2. Tap the Begin Slide Show button in the toolbar.

   The presentation begins, and for a moment the Slide Show toolbar appears, before it slides up off the top of the screen (16.9).

16.9 The Slide Show toolbar appears when you start a presentation, or when you tap at the top of the screen.

3. To advance to the next slide, swipe from right to left.

   or

   To go back a slide, swipe from left to right.

4. At the end of the slideshow, a screen appears telling you to swipe forward to exit. You can exit the show early by tapping the top of the screen, which makes the Slide Show toolbar appear, and then tap End Slide Show. You can also leave slideshow mode by pinching the screen.

Marking up a slide

If you want to highlight portions of the screen during your presentation, you can do so with an onscreen pen or marker. Follow these steps:

1. Tap the Begin Slide Show button in the toolbar.

2. While the presentation is playing, tap the top of the screen, which makes the Slide Show toolbar appear.

3. Tap the Pen icon, then draw with your finger on the screen (16.10).

   or

   To change from the default pen, tap the Pen Settings button on the toolbar (16.11). You can choose from different colors for the Pen, or you can change to the Marker. You can also clear all marks by tapping Clear All.

▶ **TIP** Sometimes it's useful to blank the screen during your presentation, perhaps during a break or so the audience doesn't get distracted while you're answering a question. You can turn the screen to black by tapping the Blank Screen button in the toolbar; tapping it again returns to your presentation.

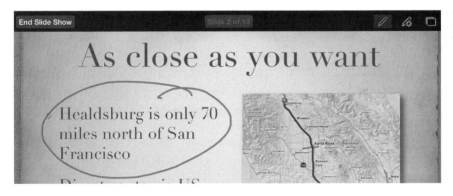

16.10 Use your finger to draw a pen mark on the screen.

16.11 The Pen Settings popover allows you to switch from the Pen to the Marker, change the markup color, or clear all marks.

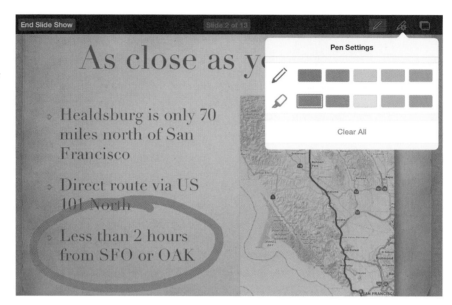

CHAPTER 17

Working with OneNote

OneNote is Office 365's note-taking application. OneNote lets you create, organize, and synchronize *notes* between your different devices. We usually think of a note as text, but in OneNote a note can be almost anything: text, whether it be a single line or several pages; a table; an image that you import or shoot with your iOS device's camera; or a link to a Web page.

An interesting thing about OneNote for iPad is that it is entirely free to download from the App Store and use: you don't need an Office 365 subscription. All you need is a free Microsoft Account and access to your free OneDrive space (though of course you get more space with a paid subscription). Your OneNote notebooks automatically and constantly synchronize between all of your devices that run OneNote, whether that be your iPad, your Macs or Windows machines, or your Windows tablets. There is even a separate OneNote app for iPhone, which is especially useful for capturing notes on the go.

In this chapter, you'll learn about the OneNote interface, how to get started capturing notes, how to style notes, and how to share your notes with other people.

Understanding OneNote

At first glance, OneNote has a similar look to the other Office 365 apps (17.1). At the top of the screen you'll find the Ribbon, which you use to format your notes, insert different note types, and change your view of your note pages. Below the Ribbon is a bar with the notebook's *section tabs*. Just as you might divide your paper notebook into tabbed sections, so you can with OneNote. Within each section, you can have as many pages as you want, which appear in the *pages pane* to the right. Chapter 18 is devoted to organizing your information with OneNote, so you'll find much more about using notebooks, sections, and pages there.

Ribbon

Section tabs
Notebook switcher

Page area

Pages pane

17.1 OneNote's interface is specialized for taking notes, but it still looks similar to the other Office apps.

You insert your notes in the *page area*. Every OneNote page goes on forever both vertically and horizontally; there's no inherent page size. Each note you create appears within a separate box on the page, and you can have as many notes on a single page as you wish. On versions of OneNote other than the iPad, you can also arrange different note types on the page however you want. In 17.1, the picture of the windup toy is in one note box, and the description pasted from Wikipedia is in another note box containing text placed and resized next to the picture.

If you are a Windows user and you have OneNote 2010 or OneNote 2013 notebooks you want to share with your iPad, you have to put the Windows notebook files on OneDrive. OneNote 2007 notebooks aren't supported, so you'll have to convert them with OneNote 2013 before you can use them on the iPad.

Unlike on Windows, a OneNote "document" doesn't live on Macs at all. Instead, it resides on a OneDrive server and is automatically synchronized whenever you have Internet access. From one standpoint, that's a good thing because your documents are constantly and seamlessly being backed up to the cloud. But on the other hand, your OneNote files are never available to you as standard documents on your machine; they are only on Microsoft's OneDrive servers. Inside the local OneDrive folder on your Mac, there is a "document" for each OneNote notebook you have, but it doesn't contain any of your OneNote data. It is merely a file containing the URL pointing to your online data.

OneNote does maintain a cache of local user data on the Mac for circumstances when Internet connectivity is down, but it is buried deep in a hidden, difficult to access folder. Personally, I don't like the idea of my data being physically unavailable to me. I want to know I can do my own backups on data important to me. And for many users, especially in the corporate environment, this is a deal breaker, because business reasons prevent them from using any cloud-based storage.

Most of the time, changes you make on the iPad, presuming that you have an Internet connection, appear on other platforms within a minute. You can work off-line with OneNote for iPad, and any changes you make are cached and will automatically sync as soon as you are back online.

▶ **NOTE** With the version of OneNote that was current when I wrote this book, you could not print from OneNote on iPad or iPhone.

As with any of the Office for iPad apps, you can pinch or spread your fingers in the page area to zoom in or out of the page. Because it is often useful with a note-taking app to have as much screen real estate as possible for your notes, OneNote allows you to hide most of its interface. Simply tap the Full Screen icon at the right end of the Ribbon (17.2), and OneNote hides most of the Ribbon, the section tabs, and the pages pane (17.3).

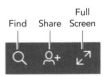

Find   Share   Full Screen

17.2 Use the Full Screen icon to get more space for your notes.

Capturing Notes

When you create a new notebook, it appears with a single section, cleverly titled "New Section 1." We'll go into more detail on working with sections in Chapter 18, so for now we'll create your first note, a text note. Simply tap anywhere in the page area, and a note box appears. Type into the note box (17.4). When you are done, tap anywhere outside the note box, and voila, your first note is complete. Anywhere you tap on a OneNote page can be the location of a box, with the exception of the very top of the page where there is a title area.

If you look at the pages pane, you'll see that by default, the name of the page is the first couple of words of the text note. You probably want something a little more useful, so let's rename the page. If you scroll up to the top of the page, you'll see that OneNote automatically date- and time-stamped the page with the creation date of the first note box, and there's a blank area above that. Tap there, and type in what you want the page title to be (17.5). As you do so, the name of the page in the pages pane changes as well.

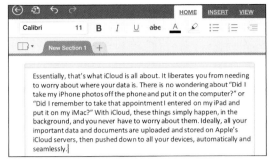

17.4 You can type or paste text into a note box, which can go anywhere on the page.

17.5 Enter the page title at the top of the page.

▶ **NOTE** A serious limitation of OneNote for iPad is that you cannot move notes between sections within the same notebook, or between notebooks. You must do that with the Windows or Mac versions. In fact, you cannot even select note boxes on the iPad once you create them; you can only select and modify their contents. That means that once you have created a note, you can't move it around the page to better arrange your notes. Again, you can turn to the Windows or Mac versions for that.

Unsupported Items on OneNote for iPad

OneNote for iPad is still very much a work in progress, and it doesn't have all the features or support all the note types from OneNote for Windows and Mac. Examples of unsupported note types and features are:

- Audio and video clips.

- Notes created with electronic "ink"—that is to say, created by drawing, handwriting, or with a stylus.

- Paragraphs that contain math equations.

- Text notes that contain pasted HTML.

- You can't password-protect sections.

- You can't embed other Microsoft Office files in notes.

Capturing image notes

Besides text, you can insert pictures from your photo library or newly captured images from your iPad's camera. The process for both is similar. Follow these steps:

1. On the page where you want the image note to appear, tap to set the insertion point.

2. On the Insert tab of the Ribbon (17.6), do one of the following:

   - To select an image from your photo library, tap Pictures. The Photos popover appears, with your shared photo albums (17.7). Tap to select a photo album, then tap the picture you want from the album.

   - To shoot a new picture with your device's camera, tap Camera, which displays a camera preview. Tap the onscreen button to snap your picture.

17.6 Use the Insert tab of the Ribbon to add images, tables, hyperlinks, and automatic dates to your pages.

17.7 The Photos popover gives you access to all your shared photo albums.

In either case, the picture appears in the picture editor (17.8).

3. In the picture editor, you can choose to apply three different sorts of filters to your image (Whiteboard, Photo, and Document), you may crop the document, or you can accept it.

   If you shot a picture of a document (you don't have to shoot it very carefully), a feature called Office Lens automatically tries to crop, rotate, and enhance the image quality (using the Document filter) so as to get the best result for your document (17.9). It often works pretty well.

17.8 Use the picture editor to filter and crop your image.

Cancel   Filters   Crop Accept

17.9 The Office Lens feature allow you to shoot a document loosely (left), which will be straightened and enhanced for better readability (right).

4. If you like the result of your image, tap the checkmark Accept icon, and the image appears in your OneNote page.

▶ **NOTE** The crop tool in OneNote is one of the oddest graphic editing tools I have ever encountered in any program. When you invoke it, it gives you editing handles at the four corners of the image, and moving the handles crops the image, as expected. But unlike crop tools in other programs, when you move OneNote's cropping handles independently, the resulting crop doesn't just cut off parts of the image, it geometrically distorts the picture, sometimes drastically. It's unclear if this is a bug or a feature, but you'll get better results cropping photos from your photo library in another image editor before you insert it into OneNote.

Inserting tables

Tables can be an important part of note taking, and you can insert tables into your OneNote pages, and even do some rudimentary calculations in the tables. Working with tables in OneNote is much easier if you are using an external Bluetooth keyboard, but they can be used with the onscreen keyboard, as well. Let's go through both methods.

To create a table when you are using an external Bluetooth keyboard, simply tap the screen to create a text box and type the information you want in the first cell of your table. Then press the Tab key on the keyboard and OneNote creates a new cell in the table. Repeat the process, pressing Tab for each column of the table, and when you are done, press the Return key, which creates the second line of the table (17.10). You can then continue typing, pressing Tab and Return as needed to fill out your table. You can move around the table by using the arrow keys on the keyboard.

If you don't have an external Bluetooth keyboard, tap the screen to create a text box, then choose Table from the Insert tab of the Ribbon (see 17.6). The contextual Table tab appears in the Ribbon (17.11). Use the items on this tab to select, insert, or delete cells, rows, columns, or the entire table. Because the onscreen keyboard doesn't have a Tab key, tap in the table to move from one cell to another.

OneNote supports simple calculations inside tables, though it's not quite what you would expect if you are used to Excel. In a given table cell you can type a simple equation, using the four arithmetic operators (+, -, *, /), then press the equals key (=). The result of the calculation appears in the cell along with the rest of the equation (17.12). You can't refer to other cells, as you could in Excel, and things like Excel functions aren't supported.

▶ **TIP** Actually, you aren't limited to adding these sorts of calculations only in table cells; you can do them in any text box, though of course they tend to make the most sense in the context of a table.

Home Sales	Q1	Q2	Q3	Q4

17.10 It's easy to add a table to your notes, especially if you happen to be using an external Bluetooth keyboard.

17.11 Whenever you create a table, the contextual Table tab appears in the Ribbon.

Let's do	a calculation:	(17+3)/2=10

17.12 You can do calculations inside tables in OneNote.

Inserting to-do lists

OneNote supports as a native data type the to-do list, which is a text list that includes checkboxes next to each item. Initially you create unchecked items in the list, then you can go back and check them off at your leisure. To create a to-do list, follow these steps:

1. Tap to place the insertion point anywhere on a OneNote page, creating a new note box for text.

2. (Optional) Type a title for your to-do list, then press the Return key.

3. Type the first item in your list.

4. On the Home tab of the Ribbon, tap the To Do icon (17.13).

   Next to the item you typed, a checkbox appears.

5. Press Return, then type the rest of the items in your list. A checkbox will accompany each item. To stop checkboxes from appearing but still continue typing in the same text box, press the Return key twice. When you are done with your list, each item will have a check box (17.14). Return to the list as needed and tap to check off items.

17.13 You can make any item part of a to do list.

17.14 Each item in your to do list has a checkbox (left), which you can check off at any time (right).

Things to do

☐ Water the lawn
☐ Wash the car
☐ Deposit huge royalty checks
☐ Live life of well-deserved luxury

Things to do

☑ Water the lawn
☑ Wash the car
☐ Deposit huge royalty checks
☐ Live life of well-deserved luxury

Styling Text Notes

You use the Home tab of the Ribbon to style text on your OneNote pages (17.15). To style text, follow these steps:

1. Select the text you want to style.

2. Use the controls in the Home tab of the Ribbon to make your desired changes. The text changes as you command.

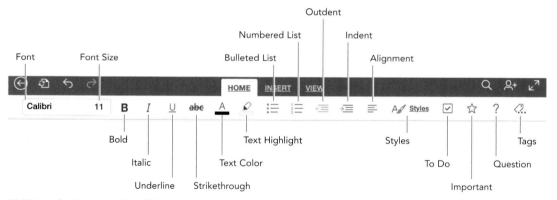

17.15 Use the Home tab of the Ribbon to style your text.

Most of the controls are familiar from the other Office for iPad apps, though a few are worthy of special mention. The text features in OneNote can't rival Microsoft Word, but the styles available in the Styles popover are designed to be compatible with standard Word styles. You'll find the familiar Heading 1 through Heading 6, as well as styles such as Page Title and Normal. Notes with these styles will look similar whether the text of the note is in OneNote or Word.

Besides the To Do formatting choice discussed earlier, OneNote also has two other common tags for notes: Important and Question. You can add these and the other tags that appear in the Tags popover on the Home tab of the Ribbon to your notes (17.16). In the Windows version of OneNote, you can search and find notes based on their tags, a feature that will presumably be coming in the future to the Mac and iPad versions of OneNote.

17.16 You can apply any of these tags to notes in OneNote. This list of tags was taken from the Mac version because it was easier to see, but the tags are the same.

Sharing from OneNote

You can share two things from OneNote: individual pages, which you can share via email (after automatic conversion to a PDF); and entire notebooks, which can only be shared on the Web.

You can share your notebooks with other people in two ways. First, you can tap the Share icon next to a notebook in the Notebooks list of the file manager. You share the notebook by choosing Email as Link from the resulting popover, which creates an email with a link to the document. You can choose to allow the recipient to View Only or View and Edit the document. In either case, the link opens the notebook in the recipient's default browser in OneNote Online.

Tapping the Share icon in the Home tab of the Ribbon (17.17) allows you to share the notebook in one of three ways:

- **Email as Link** creates an email with a link to the notebook on One-Drive. This has the same effect as sharing the whole notebook in the file manager.

- **Email Page** creates an email with only the current page as a PDF attachment to the email. The page is sent as an email directly from your iPad.

- **Copy Link** is similar to Email as Link, except that it only gets a link and doesn't create an email. It's useful for when you want to include a link in a Web page or social media message. It also has View Only or View and Edit options.

17.17 Use the Share popover to share your notebook or individual pages with coworkers.

CHAPTER 18

Organizing
Your Notes

There are three schools of thought when it comes to organizing and finding information. One school says don't bother organizing your information, but simply search for what you want when you need it and rely on the power of the search engine to correctly retrieve your data. This is the approach taken by Google's Gmail, which substitutes fast searching for filing e-mails away in folders. A second approach augments searching the contents of your data with tags that you apply to the different data documents. You create your own set of tags, which serve as personalized reminders of your data categories. This approach is espoused by Evernote, a popular competitor to OneNote.

Yet a third method of organization, and the one used by OneNote, is to rely on you to organize the data in ways that make sense to you. Much like an electronic version of old-fashioned paper note-books, OneNote data is organized first into *notebooks*, then into tabbed *sections* within a notebook, and finally into *pages* within each section. Here is where the analogy to the paper notebooks breaks down a bit, because OneNote also allows you to create *subpages* (though not on the iPad).

In this chapter, you'll see how to organize your information by creating new notebooks and sections, how to create and delete new pages, and how to use OneNote to find information in your notebooks.

Working with Notebooks

One of the major benefits of OneNote for many people is that it looks so similar to a real paper notebook simply translated to the screen. For those of us old enough to remember going through elementary and junior high school with Trapper Keepers and Pee Chee folders filled with loose-leaf notebook paper, the organizational paradigm is familiar and natural.

Dealing with OneNote's Limitations

A big problem with OneNote on the iPad is that it is the newest member of the family and just isn't as powerful as OneNote for Windows, Mac, or OneNote Online. You can do things with any of those versions that you simply can't do with OneNote for iPad (at least not yet). But OneNote for iPad is improving and adding more features, and the rate of change is accelerating now that the rest of the Office 365 suite is available for iPad. OneNote's original version for iPad, released in December 2011, was widely panned by reviewers as lacking so many features compared to its Windows brethren that it was almost unusable. But the version released in March 2014 was not only completely redesigned for iOS 7, it added features that brought it a long ways towards parity with its other versions.

In the meantime, if you need to do things with OneNote that simply aren't supported on OneNote for iPad (and some of those things are very useful, like creating subpages) just open your OneNote notebook on a Mac, in your browser, or on a Windows PC and make the changes you want. It's perfectly okay to use the iPad mainly as a data capture device and to use OneNote running on other platforms to pretty up and better organize your work.

You don't need to worry about features that are supported by other versions of OneNote but not by OneNote for iPad. For example, I recorded an audio note on OneNote for Windows, a feature that isn't supported for OneNote for iPad or Mac. After syncing through OneDrive, the page with the audio note shows the icon of the audio note on all devices, but if you try to play the audio on platforms that don't support that feature, you'll simply get an error message.

▶ **NOTE** For you nostalgia buffs, I happened to be reading a news story the morning I wrote this describing how Mead, the original maker of Trapper Keepers and Pee Chees, is teaming up with Kensington to reintroduce the brands as universal tablet cases that will fit 8 inch and 10 inch iPads and Android tablets.

The core of OneNote's organizational structure is the notebook. It's entirely up to you whether you want more than one notebook. For example, you could have a single notebook that encompasses all of your note-taking needs. Or you could have separate notebooks for different areas of your life, such as work, school, personal, etc. OneNote for iPad allows you to create new notebooks and switch between them on the fly.

To create a new notebook in OneNote for iPad, follow these steps:

1. At the left edge of the Ribbon, tap the Back icon (18.1).

   The file manager appears.

2. If it is not already selected, tap the Notebooks button, and any existing notebooks you have on your OneDrive appear (18.2).

3. Tap Create Notebook. In the resulting Create Notebook sheet, type the name of the new notebook, then tap Create (18.3).

Back

18.1 You get to the file manager by tapping the Back icon in the Ribbon.

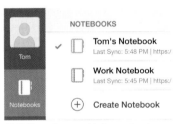

18.2 If you have multiple notebooks, they will appear on the Notebooks tab of the file manager.

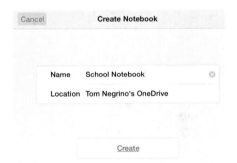

18.3 Enter the name of your new notebook.

Note that the location is fixed to being on your OneDrive. Unlike the other Office for iPad apps, you can't save a notebook privately on your iPad. You'll have to decide for yourself whether this enforced cloud storage is a privacy issue for you. However, in the event that you don't have Internet connectivity, any changes you make inside OneNote on your iPad will be automatically saved and then just as automatically synchronized when Internet connectivity and access to your OneDrive returns.

Notebook switcher Section tab New section Page title area Notebook title

18.4 A new notebook starts off with a single generic tab.

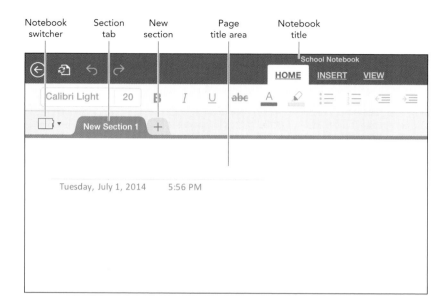

The new notebook is created, and you switch to editing mode (18.4).

You can switch between different notebooks in OneNote for iPad by tapping the Notebook Switcher at the left edge of the section tab bar. From the resulting popover (18.5), choose the notebook you want; in this popover, OneNote will also overlay syncing badges on any notebooks that it is updating from the network. If you don't currently have Internet access, OneNote will warn you by overlaying connection lost badges on the notebooks in the Notebooks popover (18.6) and will display an alert box if you lose Internet connectivity unexpectedly while working in a notebook.

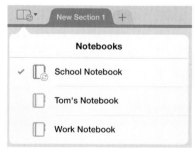

18.5 You can tell that the School Notebook is being synchronized by the badge on its icon.

18.6 OneNote lets you know when your iPad is offline with connection lost badges in the Notebooks popover,

Working with Sections

Sections are the tabs that run across the top of your notebook in the section tab bar. They are completely free form, and you can use them however you like as organizational devices. For example, if you have a School Notebook, you might want to assign it one section per class. In a work-oriented notebook, each section could be the name of a client, or if you have a variety of job responsibilities, you could assign each section to a different one of those responsibilities (e.g., Sales, Marketing, Product Support).

When a new notebook is created, OneNote populates it with a single section tab titled "New Section 1." Probably the first thing you want to do is rename that section, and you do that by double tapping the section tab, which selects the title and brings up an Edit popover (18.7). Type the new name, then tap anywhere else on the page to lock in the change.

To create a new section, tap the New Section icon in the section tab bar (see 18.4). OneNote creates a new section with a different colored tab in the section name already selected. Type the new name for the section, then tap anywhere else on the screen to save the change (18.8).

▶ **TIP** Of course, you could use the Edit popover to paste in the section names from other places within OneNote; you don't have to type them yourself.

You can also delete sections on the iPad. While double tapping on a section tab brings up the Edit popover—allowing you to cut, copy, or paste the tab name—a quick single tap on a section tab brings up a different popover allowing you to delete or rename the tab (18.9).

There are things you are going to want to do with sections that are beyond the current capabilities of OneNote for iPad (at least as it was when I wrote this book). I suggest that you instead turn to the Windows, OneNote Online, or Mac versions to accomplish these tasks; in most cases the results of operations you perform on the other platforms will appear on the iPad.

18.7 After selecting it, type in the new name for your section.

18.8 OneNote for iPad lets you create and name new sections.

18.9 You can also delete or rename sections as you wish.

For example, the Windows version of OneNote gives you the opportunity to move or copy sections; merge them with another section; create a *section group* (multiple sections that then appear as a single tab in the section bar, for example, you could group your physics and biology classes into a Science section group); change the section color; and more (18.10). You can also do these things to greater or lesser extent on the Mac or online versions, but the Windows version, being the original, has the most features.

18.10 This screenshot from OneNote's Windows version shows you the additional section options you have on that platform.

Working with Pages

18.11 Tap Add Page to add a new page to your section.

After notebooks and sections in the organizational chain comes pages. Pages are contained in a section, and you can have as many pages as you want in a section. Individual notes appear on a page, and there is no fixed size for a page. You can have as many notes on a page as you like, and placement of notes on a page is entirely free form; just tap on the page and start typing for a text note, or paste in or insert an image or table.

Adding a new page is as simple as tapping the Add Page icon at the top of the pages pane (18.11). The new page appears at the bottom of the list of pages in the pages pane, initially named Untitled Page. But at the same time the insertion point appears in the title area at the top of the page, allowing you to enter the name of the page (18.12).

18.12 Changes you make in the page title area are reflected in the pages pane.

To rename the page, select the name of the page in the page's title area and enter the new name. To delete a page, select it in the pages pane, then swipe to the left to reveal the Delete icon (18.13). Tap the Delete icon and the page is deleted without an "are you sure?" warning. However, if you made a mistake, you can get it back immediately by tapping the Undo icon in the Ribbon.

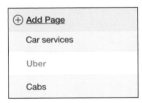
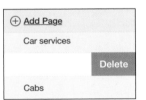

18.13 To delete a page, select it in the pages pane (left) then swipe to the left to display then tap the Delete button (right).

As with sections, you'll need to turn to other versions of OneNote to make some important and useful changes with pages. Use other versions, notably the Windows version, to rearrange pages within the same section; to move pages around by cutting, copying, or pasting them; to move or copy them directly to another section or even another notebook; or to make a page a subpage of another. You can see subpages in 18.12; the items under "Things to Do" are subpages I moved underneath the main topic using the Mac version.

▶ **TIP** One thing that (as of the time I wrote this book) you could only do with the Windows version was to display previous versions of pages, which can be immensely useful to see your changes over time.

Finding Notes

After you have a lot of your information in OneNote, you're naturally going to want to retrieve it, and the fastest way to do that is by searching for it. Follow these steps:

Search

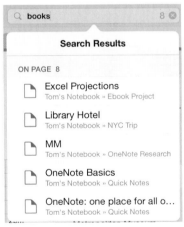

18.14 Begin searching by tapping the Search icon in the Ribbon.

1. Begin by tapping the Search icon on the right side of the Ribbon (18.14).

   The Ribbon is replaced by the Search field.

2. To decide where to search, tap the Options icon next to the search field, and choose the scope of your search from the resulting popover (18.15).

   You can choose to search the current section, the section group, the current notebook, or all notebooks.

3. Type your search term in the search field, and as you type the Search Results popover shows you the live search results, and in the search field you can see the total number of results (18.16).

▶ **NOTE** Unfortunately, you can't search for tags you may have added to notes. That handy ability exists in the Windows version of OneNote, so hopefully it will eventually make it to the iPad.

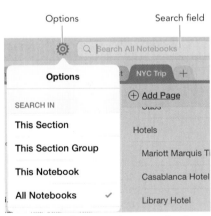

18.15 Choose the scope of your search using the Options popover.

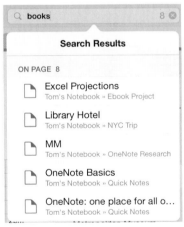

18.16 As you type your search term, the Search Results popover updates.

Index

Symbol

= (equal) sign, appearance in Excel, 153

A

Accept change button, 124
accounts
    adding people to, 5–7
    entering passwords for, 6
    signing into, 14–15, 20
    signing up for, 2
Add text box, 181
Add User button, clicking, 7
AirPlay, using for video mirroring, 199
alignment, using with OneNote, 212
animations, 191
App Store, accessing, 13
Apple TV and AirPlay, using for
    presentations, 198
apps. See also Office apps
    downloading, 2
    problems with, 7–8
AutoFill, using with Excel for iPad, 142
AutoFit, using with Excel for iPad, 143
AutoSave switch, sliding to Off, 31
AutoSum, using with Excel for iPad, 141

B

Back button, identifying, 31
Backstage, clicking Save As in, 51
Bar tab, setting, 119
Block Authors button, 124
Bold text
    OneNote for iPad, 212
    PowerPoint for iPad, 181
    Word for iPad, 110
borders, applying to worksheets, 148
Breaks popover, using, 131
bulleted lists
    OneNote for iPad, 212
    PowerPoint for iPad, 181
    Word for iPad, 110
bullets, inserting into Word, 112
Bullets popover, using in Word, 112
Business plan, subscribing to, 3

C

Camera Backup feature, 20, 89
cell formatting, moving in Excel for iPad,
    140
cell ranges, filling with series, 142
Cell Styles popover, using with Excel for
    iPad, 150
cell tools, identifying in Excel, 137
cell values, moving in Excel for iPad, 140
cells. See also Excel for iPad
    activating in Excel for iPad, 139–140
    applying color to, 148
    clearing, 140
    copying, 140
    cutting, 140
    moving, 140
    selecting and dragging, 140
Center tab, setting, 119
Center tool, 110
changes. See Track Changes feature
chart axes, switching, 167–168
chart layouts, applying, 166–167
chart styles
    changing colors, 165
    choosing, 165
    customizing, 165
    formatting, 164–166
    Monochromatic choices, 165
chart types
    changing, 163
    stacked 3D column, 163
charts
    copying and pasting, 162
    copying data for, 160–161
    creating, 160–163
    formatting, 162
    inserting, 160, 163
    moving, 162
    recommended type, 161–162
Charts popover, displaying, 163
cloud services, sharing photos on, 21
Cloud storage, 9, 15. See also storage
collaboration tools
    Accept change, 124
    Block authors, 124
    Delete comment, 124

collaboration tools (*continued*)
   Display for Review, 124
   Next change, 124
   Next comment, 124
   Preview comment, 124
   Previous change, 124
   Reject change, 124
   Track Changes, 124
column break, inserting, 133–134
columns
   adding, 132–134
   choosing number of, 133
   displaying in Excel for iPad, 136
   freezing, 145–146
   inserting in Excel for iPad, 144
   lining up in Word, 120
   selecting in Excel for iPad, 143
comments, adding, 124
Copy Link option, using, 38–39
copying
   cells in Excel for iPad, 140
   data for charts, 160–161
COUNTA function, using in Excel,
   156–157

D
Decimal Tab, setting, 119
deleted items, retrieving with
   OneDrive, 76
deleting
   files in OneDrive app, 84
   folders in OneDrive, 75–77
   sections, 219
   slides, 181
   values from rows and columns,
     143
   worksheets in Excel, 138
desktop setup, 15–17. *See also*
   Springboard
Different First Page switch, turning
   on, 122
Different Odd & Even switch,
   turning on, 122
.doc and .dot file formats, 10
.docs, .docm, and .dotx file
   formats, 10
document length, discovering,
   115–116
document versions, accessing in
   Office Online, 100

document view, resizing, 41
documents. *See also* recent
   documents; Word Online
   documents
   autosaving, 31–32
   creating, 30–31
   creating from built-in templates,
     44–48
   creating in Office Online, 94–97
   editing in Office Online, 100
   naming, 31–33, 46
   opening, 34–37
   opening in Office Online, 98–99
   pinning, 36
   printing, 40
   printing in Office Online, 99
   renaming in Office Online, 99
   saving, 31–33, 46–48
   sharing, 38–39
   sharing in Office Online,
     100–105
   storage locations, 33
   storing, 7–8
   unpinning, 36
   zooming out of, 46
Documents folder, using with
   OneDrive, 28
downloading apps, 2
downloading Office apps, 12–14
Dropbox
   photo-uploading feature, 21
   popularity of, 19

E
editing documents in Office
   Online, 100
email address, entering for
   Microsoft account, 6
Email as Attachment option, using,
   38–39
Email as Link option, using, 38–39
Excel documents, opening, 136
Excel for iPad. *See also* cells;
   functions; worksheets
   = (equal) sign, 153
   activating cells, 139–140
   active cell, 139
   adding worksheets, 136
   AutoFill, 142
   AutoFit, 143

   AutoSum, 141
   building formulas, 153–155
   cell ranges, 138
   Cell Styles popover, 150
   clearing cells and cell ranges,
     140
   clearing values, 143
   copying cells and cell ranges,
     140
   copying values, 143
   creating documents, 30–31
   cutting cells and cell ranges, 140
   cutting values, 143
   deleting values, 143
   Edit popover, 143, 152
   entering data, 140–141
   extending selections, 139–140
   external references, 158
   file formats, 10
   filling data, 142
   Formula Bar, 155–157
   freezing panes, 145–146
   Home tab of Ribbon, 137
   inserting columns, 144
   inserting rows, 144
   moving cell formatting, 140
   moving cell values, 140
   numeric keyboard, 141
   Ribbon, 41, 137
   selecting columns, 143
   selecting rows, 143
   status bar info icon, 138
   templates, 44–48
   Text Functions popover, 155
   workbooks, 136
Excel for iPad limitations
   150% view, 139
   comments, 139
   Conditional Formatting, 139
   Data Validation, 139
   macros, 139
   Pivot Tables, 139
   sorting and filtering, 139
   sparklines, 139
   splitting windows, 139
   worksheets and workbooks, 139
Excel Formulas-tab functions
   AutoSum, 154
   Calculator, 154
   Date and Time, 154

Financial, 154
Logical, 154
Lookup & Reference, 154
Math & Trigonometry, 154
More, 154
Recent, 154
Text, 154
Excel function categories
AutoSum, 154
Date and Time, 154
Financial, 154
Logical, 154
Lookup & Reference, 154
Math & Trigonometry, 154
More, 154
Recent, 154
Text, 154

F

Favorites folder, using with
OneDrive, 28
File button, identifying, 31
file formats
converting, 10
Excel, 10
PowerPoint, 10
Word, 10
file manager
Recent view, 34
using, 30–31
File sheet, 32
files. *See also* Office files
accessing, 7
deleting in OneDrive app, 84
moving in OneDrive app, 84
opening in OneDrive app,
80–82
refreshing in OneDrive app, 88
renaming in OneDrive app,
83–84
renaming on Macs, 35
sharing in OneDrive app, 87
viewing in OneDrive app, 80–82
filling data in Excel for iPad, 142
Find & Replace tool, 110
finding text in Word for iPad,
114–115
First line indent marker, dragging,
119

Flickr photo storage, 21
folders
canceling in OneDrive app, 71
deleting in OneDrive, 75–77
displaying in OneDrive, 21
moving in OneDrive, 75–77
refreshing in OneDrive app, 88
sharing in OneDrive app, 85–86
using with OneDrive app, 70–72
Font Color tool, 181
Font Size tool
OneNote for iPad, 212
PowerPoint for iPad, 181
Word for iPad, 110
Font tool
OneNote for iPad, 212
PowerPoint for iPad, 181
Word for iPad, 110
font types, using with PowerPoint,
172
footers and headers, using,
121–122
formatting popover tool, 110
Formula Bar
components of, 156
external references, 158
identifying in Excel for iPad, 136
using, 155–157
using in Excel, 136–137,
155–157
formulas
building in Excel for iPad,
153–155
versus functions, 153
identifying, 153
Free button, tapping, 13
freezing panes in Excel for iPad,
145–146
functions. *See also* Excel for iPad
COUNTA, 156–157
entering, 153
versus formulas, 153
returning arguments, 153
SUM, 153–154
using, 155

G

Google Drive website, 91
graphs. *See* charts

H

hanging indent, creating, 119
headers and footers, using,
121–122
Home plan, subscribing to, 3
Home tab of Ribbon. *See* Ribbon
Home-tab tools

I

iCloud service
for shared storage, 19
using, 8
images, adding to presentations,
187. *See also* photos
Important tool, using with
OneNote, 212
importing presentations, 170–175
importing templates. *See also*
templates
from Office 2011 for Mac, 54–56
from Office 2013 in Windows,
49–53
from Office Online, 57–64
Indent tool, 110
indents
setting, 118–119
toolbar, 181
using with OneNote, 212
inserting page numbers, 122–123
installing
Mac software, 18
OneDrive on Macs, 22–24
OneDrive on Windows, 23
Windows software, 17
Italic text
OneNote for iPad, 212
PowerPoint for iPad, 181
Word for iPad, 110

J

Justify tool, 110

L

landscape orientation, 129
Left indent marker, dragging, 118
Left Tab, setting, 119
Left tool, 110

Line Spacing tool, 110
links, sharing, 39
lists
    applying to text, 112–114
    mixing types of, 114
    multi-level, 114

M

Mac software, installing, 18
Macs
    installing OneDrive on, 22–24
    OneDrive folder, 25–26
    renaming files on, 35
margin presets, using, 128
margin settings
    Mirrored, 128
    Moderate, 128
    Narrow, 128
    Normal, 128
    Office 2003 Default, 128
    Wide, 128
Microsoft accounts
    adding people to, 5–7
    entering passwords for, 6
    signing into, 14–15, 20
    signing up for, 2
mobile device setup, downloading
        Office apps, 12–14
My Account option, accessing,
        6, 16

N

naming documents, 31–33, 46
Next change button, 124
notebooks, 44. See also OneNote
        for iPad
    accessing file manager, 217
    creating, 217
    naming, 217
    page title area, 218
    pages, 220–221
    sections, 218–220
    sharing from OneNote, 213–214
    switching between, 218
    synchronizing, 218
    titles, 218

notes. See also OneNote for iPad
    applying tags to, 213
    capturing, 206–212
    entering page title, 207
    finding, 222
    pages pane, 206
    renaming pages, 206
    typing and pasting text, 207
Number Formatting, identifying in
        Excel, 137
number values, formatting in Excel
        for iPad, 151–152
numbered lists
    OneNote for iPad, 212
    PowerPoint for iPad, 181
    Word for iPad, 110
numbers, inserting into Word, 112
numeric keyboard, using with
        Excel for iPad, 141

O

Office 365
    apps for iPad, 4
    Business plan, 3
    downloading apps, 2
    Home plan, 3
    locations, 11
    OneDrive software, 4
    Online versions, 4–5
    running on tablets, 20
    signing into, 14–15
    storage, 4
    subscribing to, 2–4
    University plan, 4
    using, 2
    versions, 4
Office apps. See also apps
    displaying search results, 13
    downloading, 12–14
    Free button, 13
Office files. See also files
    opening with OneDrive, 78–80
    viewing with OneDrive, 78–80
Office for iPad interface, 41–42
Office Online
    accessing document versions,
        100
    apps, 92
    Browse Templates button, 94

Continue button, 96
    creating documents, 94–97
    document templates, 95
    duplicating saved documents,
        57–62
    editing documents, 100
    features, 57, 91–92
    File tab, 100
    Meeting Minutes template, 95
    navigating apps, 106
    navigating services, 106
    opening documents, 98–99
    organizing templates, 60
    printing documents, 99
    renaming documents, 99
    requirements, 93
    saving templates, 62–64
    sharing documents, 100
    signing into, 93
    starting, 57
    Word, 96
Office Online document sharing
    by embedding in Web pages,
        104–105
    with link on social media,
        103–104
    via email, 102–103
OneDrive for iPad
    About section, 90
    access limitations, 8
    Account settings, 90
    Actions button, 68–69
    Camera Backup settings, 89–90
    canceling folders, 71
    creating folders, 70–72
    delays with downloads, 78
    deleting files, 84
    deleting folders, 75–77
    determining version, 90
    displaying folders in, 21
    features, 4, 19–20, 66
    file manager, 10
    file viewer, 78–80
    Items area, 68–69
    loading Camera Backup, 67
    moving files, 84
    moving folders, 75–77
    opening files, 80–82
    opening Office files, 78–80
    Recent tab, 89

refreshing files, 88
refreshing folders, 88
renaming files, 83–84
renaming folders, 73–75
returning to top level, 72
running for first time, 24–27
screen areas, 68–69
setting up on iPad, 20–21
Settings sheet, 90
Shared tab, 89
sharing files, 87
sharing folders, 85–86
Sign Out choice, 90
signing into, 66–68
Storage settings, 90
sync settings, 26
Tab bar, 68–69
toolbar, 68–69
viewing files, 80–82
viewing Office files, 78–80
OneDrive folders
benefits, 27
Documents, 28
Favorites, 28
features, 27
file sizes, 27
moving, 27
Pictures, 28
Public, 28
renaming, 27
Shared Favorites, 28
specifying location for, 25–26
OneDrive Online app, 101
OneNote for iPad. See also
notebooks, notes
capturing image notes, 208–210
capturing notes, 206
Copy Link option, 214
crop tool, 210
Email as Link option, 214
Email Page option, 214
Find icon, 205
Full Screen icon, 205–206
hiding interface, 205
Important tag, 213
inserting pictures, 208–210
inserting tables, 210–211
inserting to-do lists, 211–212
interface, 204
limitation, 207

limitations, 216, 221
notebooks, 205
Question tag, 213
Ribbon, 41
Share icon, 205
sharing from, 213–214
sharing notebooks, 213–214
styling text notes, 212–213
templates, 44
unsupported items, 207
online storage view, refreshing, 35
online templates. See Office
Online; templates
Online versions, 4–5
opening documents, 34–37
Orientation popover, 129
outdents
OneNote for iPad, 212
PowerPoint for iPad, 181
Word for iPad, 110

P
page breaks, 131–132
page direction, flipping, 129
page numbers
adding text for, 123
inserting, 122–123
page size, changing, 129
pages
adding to sections, 220–221
deleting, 221
renaming, 221
using in OneNote for iPad,
220–221
panes, freezing and unfreezing,
145–146
paper size, choosing, 129
paragraph formatting. See Ruler
paragraph marks, showing, 110,
131
paragraphs, viewing ends of, 110
password, entering for Microsoft
account, 6
photo library, using with
PowerPoint, 188
photos. See also images
sharing, 21
storing on Flickr, 21
pictures. See images; photos

Pictures folder, using with
OneDrive, 28
pinning documents, 36
placeholders, replacing in Word
Online, 96
portrait orientation, 129
PowerPoint for iPad. See also
presentations; slides
adding images, 187–189
adding tables, 185–187
Alignment popover, 183
copying styles, 183–184
creating documents, 30–31
creating shapes, 189–190
document view, 42
file formats, 10
fixing font problems, 173–175
Formatting popover, 183
image files, 172
inserting text boxes, 184–185
JPG format, 172
PNG format, 172
preflighting shows, 194–195
resizing text boxes, 182
Ribbon, 41
slide animations, 191
styling text, 181–183
templates, 44–48
PowerPoint for iPad limitations
audio clips, 173
charts, 173
comments, 173
find and replace feature, 185
manipulating pictures, 189
slide animations, 173
slide transitions, 173
Smart Art, 173, 190
video clips, 173
PowerPoint pitfalls
iOS Fonts, 172
media files, 172
Office Compatible Fonts, 172
Theme Fonts, 172
TIF files, 172
watching for, 171–172
.ppt, .pot, and .pps file formats, 10
.pptx, .pptm, .potx, and .ppsx file
formats, 10
practicing presentations, 195–196
preflighting shows, 194–195

presentations, 170–175. *See also* PowerPoint for iPad; slides
  Apple TV and AirPlay, 198
  creating on PowerPoint for iPad, 175–176
  creating slide types, 176
  direct connections, 198
  hardware connection, 197–199
  importing, 170–175
  playing, 200
  practicing, 195–196
  preflighting shows, 194–195
  preparation, 196–197
  video connections, 197–198
  video mirroring, 199
Previous change button, 124
printers, selecting, 40
printing
  changing virtual paper, 129
  documents, 40
  documents in Office Online, 99
Properties sheets, using, 37
Public folder, using with OneDrive, 28

Q

Question tool, using with OneNote, 212

R

recent documents, managing, 37. *See also* documents
Recent tab, using in OneDrive app, 89
Recent view, using in file manager, 34
recommended charts, creating, 161–162
Redo tool, 31, 110
refreshing
  files in OneDrive app, 88
  folders in OneDrive, 88
Reject change button, 124
renaming
  documents in Office Online, 99
  files in OneDrive app, 83–84
  files on Macs, 35
  folders in OneDrive, 73–75

replacing text in Word for iPad, 114–115
resizing document view, 41
Review tab. *See* Ribbon Review-tab tools
revisions, controlling in Track Changes, 125
Ribbon
  buttons in, 31
  tabs in, 41
  in Word for iPad, 108–109
Ribbon Home-tab tools
  Add text box, 181
  Alignment, 137, 212
  Bold, 110, 137, 181, 212
  Bulleted lists, 181
  bulleted lists, 110, 212
  Cell Borders, 137
  Cell Content Color, 137
  Cell Fill Color, 137
  Cell Styles, 137
  Center, 110
  Find & Replace, 110
  Font, 110, 137, 181, 212
  Font Color, 181
  Font Size, 110, 137, 181, 212
  Formatting popover, 110, 181
  Important tag, 212
  Indent, 110, 181, 212
  Insert & Delete Cells, 137
  Italic, 110, 137, 181, 212
  Justify, 110
  Left, 110
  Line Spacing, 110
  Merge Cells, 137
  Number Formatting, 137
  numbered lists, 110, 181, 212
  Outdent, 110, 181, 212
  Question tag, 212
  Redo, 110
  Right, 110
  shapes, 181
  show paragraph marks, 110–111
  Sort and Filter, 137
  Strikethrough, 212
  Styles, 110
  styles, 212
  Tags, 212
  Text alignment, 181

  Text Color, 110, 212
  Text Highlight, 110, 212
  Text styles, 181
  To Do, 212
  Underline, 110, 137, 181, 212
  Undo, 110
Ribbon Review-tab tools
  Accept change, 124
  Add comment, 124
  Block authors, 124
  Delete comment, 124
  Display for Review, 124
  Next change, 124
  Next comment, 124
  Preview comment, 124
  Previous change, 124
  Reject change, 124
  Track Changes, 124
Right indent marker, dragging, 119
Right tab, setting, 119
Right tool, 110
rows
  freezing, 145–146
  inserting in Excel for iPad, 144
  selecting in Excel for iPad, 143
Ruler. *See also* Word for iPad
  displaying, 118
  setting indents, 118–119
  setting tabs, 119–120
  using for portion of documents, 120

S

Save As dialog, using, 33, 46–47
saving documents, 31–33, 46–48
screen areas, zooming, 110
search mode, using with Word for iPad, 114–115
section breaks
  adding, 130–132
  Continuous, 131
  Even Page, 132
  Next Page, 131
  Odd Page, 132
sections
  adding pages to, 220
  deleting, 219
  using with notebooks, 218–220

shapes
  adding to slides, 189–190
  Basic Shapes, 189
  Block Arrows, 189
  Callouts, 189–190
  Equation, 189
  Flowchart, 189
  icon, 181
  Lines, 189
  Rectangles, 189
  Stars and Banners, 189
Share functions
  Copy Link, 38–39
  Discard Changes, 37
  Email as Attachment, 38–39
  Email as Link, 38–39
  Move to Cloud, 37
  Properties, 37
  Remove from Recent, 37
Shared Favorites folder, using with
  OneDrive, 28
Shared tab, using in OneDrive
  app, 89
sharing
  documents, 38–39, 100
  files in OneDrive app, 87
  folders in OneDrive app, 85–86
  links, 39
  Office Online documents,
    101–105
  from OneNote, 213–214
Show Paragraph Marks tool,
  110–111
Sign In button, locating, 5
signing into accounts, 14–15, 20
SkyDrive. See OneDrive for iPad
slide animations, 191
slide pane, shrinking slides in, 195
Slide Show toolbar icons
  Blank Screen, 200
  Pen, 200–202
  Pen Settings, 200
slide transitions
  adding, 192–194
  changing, 193
  reusing, 194
slide types, creating for
  presentations, 176
slides. See also PowerPoint for
  iPad; presentations

  adding shapes to, 189–190
  advancing to, 200
  changing order, 178–179
  cutting and pasting, 178–179
  deleting, 181
  dragging, 179
  duplicating, 179–180
  hiding, 180
  marking up, 201–202
  moving, 178–179
software. See Mac software;
  Windows software
sparklines, viewing in Excel for
  iPad, 139
Springboard, explained, 13. See
  also desktop setup
storage, 4. See also Cloud storage
storage locations, choosing for
  documents, 33
Strikethrough, using with
  OneNote, 212
styles
  applying to worksheets, 148
  using with OneNote, 212
Styles popover, using in Word, 111
Styles tool, 110
subscription benefits, displaying, 16
subscription plans, number of
  users for, 17
SUM function, using in Excel for
  iPad, 153–154

T

tables
  adding in PowerPoint for iPad,
    185–187
  inserting into OneNote,
    210–211
  rows and columns, 185
tablets, running Office on, 20
tabs
  lining up, 120
  setting with Ruler, 119–120
tags, applying to notes, 213
Tags tool, using with OneNote, 212
template libraries, 49
templates. See also importing
  templates
  accessing, 44–48

  availability, 44
  creating documents from, 44–48
  displaying, 45
  double-clicking in Backstage, 51
  explained, 43
  instruction balloons, 46
  Microsoft Word 2007, 49
  Office 2010, 49
  Office 2013, 49
  Office Online, 49
  OneNote, 44
  opening, 45
  opening in Word, 51
  organizing, 60
  using with Office Online, 95
text
  adding for page numbers, 123
  adding in Word for iPad,
    108–111
  finding in Word, 114–115
  formatting in Word for iPad, 110
  replacing in Word, 114–115
  selecting in Word for iPad, 109
  styling in PowerPoint for iPad,
    181–183
  styling in Word for iPad,
    110–111
Text alignment tool, 181
text boxes
  inserting in PowerPoint for iPad,
    184–185
  resizing in PowerPoint for iPad,
    182
Text Color tool, 110, 212
Text Highlight tool, 110, 212
text notes, styling in OneNote,
  212–213
Text styles tool, 181
titles, giving to Word Online
  documents, 97
To Do tool, using with OneNote,
  212
to-do lists, inserting into OneNote,
  211–212
Track Changes feature
  controlling revisions, 125
  Display for Review popover, 125
  on/off switch, 124
  Show Markup, 125
tracked changes, reviewing, 126

U

Underline tool
    OneNote for iPad, 212
    PowerPoint for iPad, 181
    Word for iPad, 110
Undo button, identifying, 31
University plan, subscribing to, 4
users
    adding to accounts, 7
    number per subscription plan, 17

V

versions, 4
video connections
    analog, 197
    digital, 198
    managing for presentations,
       197–198
video mirroring, controlling in
    presentations, 199
viewing screen areas, 110
virtual paper, changing, 129

W

websites
    Google Drive, 91
    Zoho Office, 91
Windows
    installing OneDrive on, 23
    OneDrive folder, 25–26
Windows software, installing, 17
word counts, getting in Word for
    iPad, 115–116
Word for iPad. *See also* Ruler
    Bullets popover, 112
    collaboration tools, 123–126
    creating documents, 30–31
    determining document length,
       115–116

displaying misspelled words, 110
document area, 108–109
editing text, 109–110
entering text, 109–110
file formats, 10
finding text, 114–115
Home tab of Ribbon, 110
inserting bullets, 112
inserting numbers, 112
lining up columns, 120
lists, 112–114
opening templates in, 51
replacing text, 114–115
Ribbon, 41–42, 108–109
search mode, 114–115
selecting text, 109
selecting words, 109
styling text, 110–111
templates, 44–48
word counts, 115–116
Word Online documents. *See also*
    documents
    document body, 96
    document name, 96
    OneDrive document path, 96
    replacing placeholder text, 96
    Ribbon, 96
    Share button, 96
    switching applications, 96
    titles, 97
    word count, 96
Word Online Web app, 97
Word styles
    applying, 111
    characters, 111
    components of document
       templates, 111
    paragraph formats, 11 1
words, selecting in Word for iPad,
    109

workbooks
    displaying in Excel for iPad, 136
    themes provided with, 148
worksheet area, 136
worksheet formatting
    appearance, 148–150
    copying, 152
    number values, 151–152
Worksheet tab, 136
worksheets. *See also* Excel for
    iPad
    adding to Excel for iPad, 136
    adding to workbooks, 138
    applying borders, 148
    applying styles, 148
    current column, 136
    current row, 136
    deleting, 138
    document title, 136
    Formula Bar, 136–137
    identifying, 136–137
    linking, 157–158
    Ribbon, 136
    selected cell, 136
    status bar info popover, 136

X

.xls and .xlt file formats, 10
.xlsx, .xlsm, and .xltx file formats,
    10

Z

Zoho Office website, 91
zooming
    out of documents, 46
    screen areas, 110, 205